The Myth That Will Not Die

No figure in the Labour movement has attracted such extremes of emotion as has James Ramsay MacDonald. Loved and almost worshipped for more than 30 years, his formation of the National Government in August 1931 incurred hatred, bitterness and contempt from those whom he had led for so long. MacDonald's career and the admiration and odium which it engendered is without parallel in British politics. Originally published in 1978, this book provides an answer to the charge that MacDonald deliberately betrayed the Labour movement by forming a coalition government with the Conservative and Liberal Parties. It examines the criticism that he ruthlessly proceeded to destroy the Labour Party in the General Election of October 1931 – an election which he pledged, only two months earlier, would not be held. Using the private papers and authorised (auto)biographies, and the Cabinet minutes of the day, this book reconstructs what really happened between August 1 and 24 1931, and accounts for the mercilessness with which MacDonald is remembered by the Labour Party.

The Myth That Will Not Die

The Formation of the National Government 1931

Humphry Berkeley

Routledge
Taylor & Francis Group

First published in 1978 by Croom Helm Ltd.

This edition first published in 2024 by Routledge
4 Park Square, Milton Park, Abingdon, Oxon, OX14 4RN
and by Routledge
605 Third Avenue, New York, NY 10158.

Routledge is an imprint of the Taylor & Francis Group, an informa business

© 1978 Humphry Berkeley

The right of Humphry Berkeley to be identified as the author of this work has been asserted by him in accordance with sections 77 and 78 of the Copyright, Designs and Patents Act 1988.

ISBN 13: 978-1-032-86338-2 (hbk)
ISBN 13: 978-1-003-52710-7 (ebk)
ISBN 13: 978-1-032-86343-6 (pbk)
Book DOI 10.4324/9781003527107

THE MYTH THAT WILL NOT DIE

THE FORMATION OF
THE NATIONAL GOVERNMENT 1931

HUMPHRY BERKELEY

CROOM HELM LONDON

©1978 Humphry Berkeley
Croom Helm Ltd, 2-10 St John's Road, London SW11

British Library Cataloguing in Publication Data

Berkeley, Humphry
    The myth that will not die.
    1. Great Britain — Politics and government
    — 1910-1936
    320.9'41'083   JN231

    ISBN 0-85664-773-X

FOR ERIC

Printed and bound in Great Britain

CONTENTS

By the same Author

THE POWER OF THE PRIME MINISTER
George Allen and Unwin 1968

CROSSING THE FLOOR
George Allen and Unwin 1972

THE LIFE AND DEATH OF ROCHESTER SNEATH
Davis-Poynter 1974

THE ODYSSEY OF ENOCH
Hamish Hamilton 1977

ACKNOWLEDGEMENTS

I wish to thank Mr Malcolm MacDonald for talking to me on many occasions at considerable length about his father's part in the formation of the National Government. I also wish to thank the following people who among others have kindly afforded me their time: Lord Boothby, Lord Shinwell, Lord Butler of Saffron Walden, Sir Oswald Mosley, Mr Robert Rhodes James MP, Sir Harold Wilson MP, Mr Kenneth Lindsay, Mr George Strauss MP and Lord Home.

I wish to thank the Keeper of the Public Record Office for his permission to reprint the Minutes of the last two Meetings of the Labour Cabinet in August 1931, and for permission to quote extracts from other Cabinet Minutes and documents.

I am deeply grateful to Mr Robin Wright for his meticulous proof reading of the manuscript of this book.

Finally, I would like to express my gratitude to my friends Mr and Mrs Fred Griffith in whose beautiful garden this book was written.

Humphry Berkeley
May 1978

INTRODUCTION

No figure in the labour movement has attracted such extremes of emotion as James Ramsay MacDonald. He was loved, almost worshipped, for more than thirty years. From 1900 until 1931 MacDonald had, more than any other single man, created the British Labour Party; he had attracted much sympathy from within the movement (although great unpopularity in the country) for his stand against the First World War. He returned in 1922 to lead the Labour Party again after his parliamentary defeat in 1918. He had become Britain's first Labour Prime Minister in 1924 and had become Prime Minister of a Labour government for a second time in 1929. Then, in August 1931, he was the main architect, or so it seemed, of the National government. He incurred hatred, bitterness, contempt and later scorn and, in the end, reluctant pity from those whom he had for so long led.

MacDonald's career and the admiration and odium which it engendered is without parallel in British democratic politics. It has made 'coalition' a polluted word in the Labour Party, even today. For most members of the Labour Party the name MacDonald is equated with that of Quisling, although the later years of his life between 1933 and 1937 might with greater accuracy and charity be compared with those of Marshal Pétain.

Few British Prime Ministers have enjoyed a relationship of undisturbed tranquillity with the party to which they belonged. At different times Churchill was hated by the Conservative and Liberal parties, and on occasion, having belonged at different times to both parties, he was more disliked by his nominal political colleagues than by his opponents. Baldwin, whose reputation among Conservatives was, except for a brief but crucial period in 1930, consistently high and never higher than when he retired, lived to hear his name reviled and his words falsified by those who earlier had been proud to serve him and who were later looking for a repository for their own guilt.

Lloyd George is considered by many to have destroyed the Liberal Party when he broke with Asquith and formed a coalition with the

Conservatives in 1916. He certainly ensured the electoral defeat of Asquith, his former chief, and of the majority of his pre-war Liberal Cabinet colleagues in the famous 'coupon' general election of 1918. Yet less than ten years later he had returned to lead the Liberal Party and, therefore, many of those for whose earlier political eclipse he had been responsible.

Few could expect so triumphant a public finale as Churchill experienced, especially since the number and scale of his misjudgements exceeded those of most of his contemporaries. His famous phrase 'I have not always been wrong' was no understatement; it was true. Yet history has a tendency to right itself in time. Lloyd George, whether he destroyed the Liberal Party or not, is commemorated as a parliamentarian by a statue in the lobby of the House of Commons, and its unveiling was not boycotted by Liberal members of Parliament. Today, the reputation of Baldwin stands higher than it did in 1947 and is, as financiers might say, on a rising market. Neville Chamberlain is remembered as a great social reformer as well as the Man of Munich. Anthony Eden, in the same way, enjoys a reputation as a distinguished Foreign Secretary which has not been completely overshadowed by the Suez fiasco. Only Ramsay MacDonald, among twentieth-century prime ministers, is remembered by the Labour Party, which he served and dominated for so long, without a trace of mercy.

This book is not a biography of Ramsay MacDonald. That task has been admirably fulfilled by David Marquand, in one of the finest biographies of recent years. I have set myself a more modest but no less necessary task — to provide, as far as it is historically possible, an answer to the charge that MacDonald deliberately and cynically betrayed the labour movement by his formation in August 1931 of the National government in co-operation with the Conservative and Liberal parties, whose leading figures were, so his accusers have said, more congenial to him than the members of his own party; and also to examine the further criticism that he then ruthlessly proceeded to destroy the Labour Party in the general election of October 1931 — an election which, only two months earlier, he had pledged would not be held. Luckily the private papers and authorised biographies or autobiographies of those who were principally concerned in the formation of the National government are now available. The Cabinet minutes of the day are now available in the Public Record Office. I have tried to reconstruct what really happened between 1 August and 24 August 1931 and have made full use of all available documentary evidence of that time. A bibliography is provided at the end of the book.

DRAMATIS PERSONAE

King George V (1865-1936) Prince of Wales 1901-10; King 1910-36.

James Ramsay MacDonald (1866-1937) Leader of the Labour Party 1911-14 and 1922-31; Prime Minister and Foreign Secretary 1924; Prime Minister of the Labour government 1929-31; Prime Minister of the National government 1931-5; Lord President of the Council 1935-7.

Stanley Baldwin (1867-1947) Conservative MP 1908-37; Financial Secretary to the Treasury 1917-21; President of the Board of Trade 1921-2; Chancellor of the Exchequer 1922-3; Conservative Prime Minister 1923-4, 1924-9, 1935-7; Lord President of the Council 1931-5; Lord Privy Seal 1932-4.

David Lloyd George (1863-1945) Liberal MP 1890-1945; Chancellor of the Exchequer 1908-15; Minister of Munitions 1915-16; Secretary of State for War 1916; Prime Minister 1916-22; Deputy Leader of the Liberal Party 1924-6; Leader of the Liberal Party 1926-31.

Philip Snowden (1864-1937) Labour MP 1906-31; Chancellor of the Exchequer 1924, 1929-31; Lord Privy Seal 1931-2 in National government.

Arthur Henderson (1864-1935) Secretary of the Labour Party 1911-34; President of the Board of Education 1915-16; Member of the War Cabinet 1916-17; Home Secretary 1924; Foreign Secretary 1929-31; Leader of the Labour Party in succession to MacDonald August-October 1931.

Neville Chamberlain (1869-1940) Conservative MP 1918-40; Postmaster General 1922-3; Paymaster General 1923; Minister of Health 1923, 1924-9, 1931; Chancellor of the Exchequer 1923-4, 1931-7; Prime Minister 1937-40; Lord President of the Council 1940.

Herbert Samuel (1870-1963) Liberal MP 1902-18, 1929-35; President of the Local Government Board 1914-15; Postmaster General 1915-16; Home Secretary 1916, 1931-2; Leader of the Liberal Party 1931-5; joined National government 1931.

John Henry Thomas (1874-1949) Labour MP 1910-36; General Secretary, National Union of Railwaymen 1917-31; Colonial Secretary 1924, 1935-6; Lord Privy Seal 1929-30; Dominions Secretary 1930-5; joined National government 1931.

Samuel Hoare (1880-1959) Conservative MP 1910-44; Secretary of State for Air 1922-4, 1924-9, 1940; Secretary of State for India 1931-5; Foreign Secretary 1935; First Lord of the Admiralty 1936-7; Home Secretary 1937-9; Lord Privy Seal 1939-40; joined National government 1931.

John Simon (1873-1954) Liberal MP 1906-18, 1922-40; Attorney-General 1913-15; Home Secretary 1915-16, 1935-7; Foreign Secretary October 1931-5; Chancellor of the Exchequer 1937-40; Lord Chancellor 1940-5; joined National government October 1931; Leader of the Liberal Party 1931-40.

Winston Spencer Churchill (1874-1965) Conservative MP 1900-6; Liberal MP 1906-22; Conservative MP 1924-64; President of Trade 1908-10; Minister of Munitions 1917-18, Secretary for War 1918-21; Secretary for the Colonies 1921-2; Chancellor of the Exchequer 1924-9; Prime Minister 1940-5, 1951-5.

William Graham Labour MP 1918-31; President of the Board of Trade 1929-31.

Arthur Greenwood (1880-1954) Labour MP 1922-3, 1932-54; Minister of Health 1929-31; Minister without Portfolio 1940-2; Lord Privy Seal 1945-7.

Herbert Morrison (1888-1965) Labour MP 1923-24, 1929-31, 1935-6; Minister of Transport 1929-31; Minister of Supply 1940; Home Secretary and Minister for Home Security 1940-5; Lord President of the Council 1945-51; Foreign Secretary 1951.

Oswald Mosley (b. 1896) Conservative MP 1918-22; Independent MP 1922-4; Labour MP 1926-31; Chancellor of the Duchy of Lancaster 1929-30; Founder, British Union of Fascists; interned during Second World War.

1 THE CAST

The month of August 1931 was the most extraordinary period in British politics of modern times. On 1 August the Labour government was in office. It was a minority government, with more seats than any other party, and dependent upon Liberal votes in Parliament to keep it in power. It had been in office for just over two years and had signally failed to deal with the most obstinate, and domestically most important, problem of long-term unemployment. But to the ordinary spectator of politics there was no reason to believe that the Labour government would not continue to remain in office for a considerable period.

The political leaders of the three major parties were only too aware of world economic conditions. Those had taken the form of an unprecedented slump which had not bypassed Great Britain. One question and one only must be asked. On 1 August 1931, did any of the participants in the extraordinary sequence of events which led to the formation of a National government less than four weeks later either plan, or even foresee, what was to take place?

One must first determine who, apart from Ramsay MacDonald, played a central part in these events, why they behaved as they did, and what kind of people they were; and, as far as possible, attribute to each of the main figures the most likely motive for his actions.

The principal performers in this drama have already been listed in the 'Dramatis Personae'; but it is, perhaps, necessary to name three of them who were not involved. Each was a national figure: one was an ex-Prime Minister, another a future Prime Minister, and the third has frequently been described as the only person of his generation whose ability was such that he could have become Prime Minister of a Conservative or a Labour government. They were David Lloyd George, Winston Churchill and Oswald Mosley. If any, or all three, of these men had played a central role in the events of August 1931, the outcome might have been dramatically different. Each, however, was totally precluded from playing any part.

Lloyd George was the official Leader of the Liberal Party, which had won 59 seats in the 1929 general election. He had been Britain's wartime leader, and Prime Minister from 1916 to 1922. Through ousting Asquith from the premiership in 1916 he had split the Liberal Party, which later became uneasily reunited under his leadership in 1926. In August 1931, however, he underwent a serious operation which forced him to appoint Sir Herbert Samuel acting Leader of his party. It is true that he was, more than once, visited at his bedside, but he was in no condition to make any impact on the course of events until after the National government had been formed.

Winston Churchill had sat in Parliament as a Conservative, a Liberal and then as a Conservative again. He had been Chancellor of the Exchequer in the Conservative government from 1924 to 1929. He had held many Cabinet posts as a Liberal, including that of First Lord of the Admiralty from 1911 to 1915. But his judgement was suspect, and in particular he was widely blamed for the Dardanelles disaster in 1915. In 1930 he had fallen out seriously with his Conservative colleagues and had resigned from the Conservative front bench because he disagreed fundamentally and violently with the India policy. This was the subject of bipartisan policy, determined in the last resort by Ramsay MacDonald and Stanley Baldwin. Churchill had only a handful of supporters on the extreme right wing of the Conservative Party.

Sir Oswald Mosley, probably the only politician with the imagination, intellect and drive to alleviate the problem of unemployment, had resigned from the Labour government in May 1930 and had formed the New Party which had only four members in Parliament, two of whom were himself and his wife. His subsequent actions are well known. They were those of a rash and deeply misguided man. Mosley could have been a great leader of this country, ranked with Cromwell, Chatham, the Younger Pitt, Lloyd George and Churchill. It is not merely his tragedy but that of our nation that, when spurned by Whitehall, Westminster and Fleet Street, he ceased to be fastidious about the company he kept or scrupulous about the methods through which he aimed to achieve power. Whilst it is possible to accept his deep sense of patriotism, by 1939 he owed allegiance to a brand of society in which many, including myself, would have found it impossible to live. In 1945, at the age of forty-nine, he could have become Labour's greatest Prime Minister. He was richly endowed with most of the qualities required;

yet he lacked three which are essential components of the complete man: patience, humility and judgement. By 1931 he was discredited and, a few years later, politically ruined. By a strange sequence of unrelated coincidences these three most dynamic figures in British public life were excluded from playing any role in the 1931 crisis.

The principal figures were King George V, Ramsay MacDonald, Philip Snowden, Stanley Baldwin, Neville Chamberlain, Sir Samuel Hoare, Sir Herbert Samuel and Arthur Henderson. J.H. Thomas, Sir Philip Cunliffe-Lister, Lord Reading and J.R. Clynes played subsidiary roles which were not sufficiently important to merit detailed examination.

King George V had been on the throne for 21 years. He was 66 years old and two years earlier had nearly died of a serious illness from which he never fully recovered. He was a man of conservative views with the strictest sense of constitutional propriety. He was in no sense opposed to the Labour government and, indeed, had formed the highest regard and affection for Ramsay MacDonald, who was undoubtedly the favourite Prime Minister of his reign.

When he first appointed Ramsay MacDonald Prime Minister in 1924, King George V wrote in his diary: 'I had an hour's talk with him, he impressed me very much; he wishes to do the right thing. Today 23 years ago dear Grandmama [Queen Victoria] died. I wonder what she would have thought of a Labour government!' J.R. Clynes, the Deputy Leader of the Labour Party, who became Lord Privy Seal in the first Labour government, wrote of the King in his memoirs:

He gave us invaluable guidance from his deep experience to help us in the difficult time before us, when we should become his principal Ministers. I had expected to find him unbending; instead he was kindness and sympathy itself. Before he gave us leave to go, he made an appeal to us that I have never forgotten: 'The immediate future of my people and their whole happiness is in your hands, gentlemen. They depend upon your prudence and sagacity.'

The King was, perhaps, over-concerned with somewhat trivial matters, such as whether Ministers would wear court dress at levees — which they agreed to do. On the other hand, the King, at first sight, liked the extreme Clydeside left-winger John Wheatley, who was Minister of Health in the first Labour government. The King noted in his diary for 22 February 1924: 'Received Mr Wheatley, the Minister of Health. He is an extreme socialist and comes from Glasgow. I had a very interesting conversation with him.' He later remarked of his conversation with Wheatley: 'I should have felt exactly as he does if I had had his sort of childhood.'

Malcolm MacDonald recalls in his essay on his father in his book *Titans and Others* that King George V, who was concerned at the horrified hostility among large sections of the British public at the advent of a Labour government, decided

> to restore confidence by demonstrating his own trust in the New Administration. He took the unprecedented step of giving a State Banquet at Buckingham Palace in honour of the new Prime Minister and the group of ex-coalminers, ex-railwaymen and others, mostly ex-manual workers, who were to be his Cabinet team.

The main concern of King George V in August 1931 was that government should be carried on in a serious national crisis with the maximum degree of unity among his people.

The complexities of Ramsay MacDonald's character were considerable. His aloofness, arrogance, so-called snobbery and his preference for the company of high-born people were resented by members of the Labour Party as diverse as Beatrice Webb, Arthur Henderson and the Clydesiders. This resentment, at least on the part of Beatrice Webb, was, almost until the end, mixed with ambivalent and reluctant admiration. On 15 February 1924, shortly after MacDonald became Prime Minister for the first time, a post which he combined with that of Foreign Secretary, Beatrice Webb wrote in her diary:

> The Foreign Office is far too pleased with MacDonald. They say 'They have got rid of a cad in Curzon and found a Gentleman in MacDonald', and of course that is the danger. J.R.M. is a born aristocrat and he will tend to surround himself with 'well bred men' — another Balfour! but with the revolutionary tradition.

A month later she wrote:

> The P.M. is unapproachable by Henderson who is responsible for the
> Labour Party organisation in the Country; and apparently by Clynes
> the Leader of the House. 'No. 10 and No. 11 [where Clynes lived]
> see no more of each other,' said Henderson to me, 'than if they slept
> and ate a hundred miles apart' and 'What interests me as a student
> of the British Constitution is the unlimited autocracy of the British
> P.M. – if he chooses to be an autocrat or slips into it through
> inertia or dislike of discussion. It was MacDonald alone who would
> determine who should be in his Cabinet; it is MacDonald who alone
> is determining what the Parliamentary Labour Party shall stand for
> in the Country.'

Mrs Webb appeared to think that a Labour Prime Minister should or
could behave differently from one of his Conservative or Liberal
predecessors. It is doubtful whether she would have made the same
complaint now after the Labour premierships of Attlee, Harold Wilson
and James Callaghan.

Early in 1924, during MacDonald's first period as Prime Minister,
Beatrice Webb began to question his socialist beliefs:

> And it is clear that the P.M. is 'playing up' towards the formation
> of a Centre Party . . . today he realises that the Liberal Party is dead;
> so he is attracting, by his newly-won prestige and personal magne-
> tism, the Conservative collectivist element . . . I do not accuse him of
> treachery: for he never was a Socialist, either revolutionary like
> Lansbury or administrative like the Webbs . . . But where he has
> lacked integrity is in posing as a Socialist and occasionally using
> revolutionary jargon . . . But it hurts my pride to see the Fabian
> Policy of permeation 'guyed' by MacDonald. Yet as a political
> performer he is showing himself a consummate artist. We never
> realised that he had genius in this direction.

In writing in such terms about MacDonald, within two months of his
becoming Prime Minister for the first time, Beatrice Webb shows considerable perception of his character and beliefs, but, of course, she

does not say, nor is there any indication that in 1924 she believed that he would abandon the Labour Party for the Conservative Party.

Beatrice Webb continued to be critical about the company which MacDonald kept during his period in opposition again between 1924 and 1929, and also during his second term as Labour Prime Minister from 1929 to 1931. At the Trades Union Congress of 1926 she wrote:

> He was particularly gracious to us; came to our table and took us into his private sitting room. Immaculately groomed and perfectly tailored — too deliberately so for artistic effect — it made him look commonplace — he went out of his way to tell me that he was going on to stay with Mrs Biddulph near Cirencester, 'The Honourable Mrs Biddulph' he added, and then described her as a patron of good English craftsmanship in furniture. 'Then I am going to stay at' — (I forget the name of the place) 'with the Princess Hartsfelt (?). She was a Cunningham you know. Do you know her? A remarkable woman.'

At the Labour Party Conference of 1926 Beatrice Webb writes:

> 'J.R.M. is not a snob' said that charming boy de la Warr [Earl de la Warr, later Conservative Postmaster General but then a member of the Labour Party] 'but he genuinely prefers the aristocrat to the proletarian as every day associates.'

She later quotes from *The Times* of September 1929 when MacDonald was again Prime Minister.

> The Prime Minister left Dunrobin Castle yesterday after his visit to the Duke and Duchess of Sutherland for Loch Choir, near Lairg, where he will be the guest of the Marquess and Marchioness of Londonderry. It is understood that he will return to Lossiemouth today and will go to Balmoral tomorrow. The return journey will be made on Monday and it is understood that he will leave Lossiemouth for London on Tuesday.

Beatrice Webb adds, 'Alas, Alas Balmoral is inevitable; but why the castles of the wealthiest, most aristocratic, most reactionary and by no means the most intellectual of the Conservative Party?' As we shall see, when the 1931 crisis approached, the deep-rooted mistrust which Beatrice Webb felt at Ramsay MacDonald's social relationships with members of the aristocracy and members of the Conservative Party, taken together with her correct diagnosis of the imprecise nature of MacDonald's socialist beliefs, led her to make what the author believes to be the incorrect assumption that MacDonald had decided to break with the Labour Party some considerable time before the formation of the National government on 24 August 1931. Beatrice Webb was not alone in criticising the social circle in which MacDonald chose to move.

In August 1925 Arthur Henderson, Home Secretary in the first Labour government and General Secretary of the Labour Party, complained about MacDonald's 'exclusive association with the smart set'. Philip Snowden, Chancellor of the Exchequer in the Labour governments of 1924 and 1929-31 and also briefly in the National government, wrote in his autobiography of the resignation of Sir Oswald Mosley.

> I can understand the working class Socialist, who knows something of the hardship of working class life, sometimes expressing bitter feelings about the class which he regards as his exploiters, but such things coming from a man like Oswald Mosley, who enjoys all the luxuries which his wealth and social position can command, give me a feeling of nausea. Mr MacDonald warmly welcomed Mosley into the Labour Party. An intimate social relationship was established such as never existed between Mr MacDonald and the plebeian members of the Labour Party.

In September 1929 Beatrice Webb wrote in her diary: 'The P.M. invites none of these colleagues [Henderson, Snowden, Thomas and Clynes] to Chequers — but he does invite smart Society dames whom he meets casually.' It was left to Snowden to record MacDonald's celebrated remark, on 24 August 1931, the day on which the National government was formed: 'Yes, tomorrow every Duchess in London will be wanting to kiss me.' It was, however, Mrs Snowden who once confessed that she did not need to enlarge her circle of friends since she had quite enough of these among the female members of the royal family.

There is no doubt that the social life of Ramsay MacDonald contributed greatly to the theory that, even as early as his first period as Prime Minister in 1924, he had been suborned by the Conservative Party. His close relationship with the Marchioness of Londonderry was viewed with particular suspicion. It was never seriously alleged that their relationship had any sexual content, but it was sufficiently intimate for Baldwin's biographers (Keith Middlemas and John Barnes) to state that when the National Cabinet was formed in 1931 by MacDonald, Lord Londonderry 'owed his promotion to MacDonald rather than Baldwin'. Four years later Sir John Davidson (later Viscount Davidson), Baldwin's closest confidant and friend, was to write of Lord Londonderry's removal from the post of Secretary of State for Air by Baldwin in June 1935: 'He owed his preferment really to the fact that Ramsay MacDonald greatly enjoyed standing at the top of the great staircase in Londonderry House as the First Minister of the Crown in full evening dress.'

It is hardly surprising that a Labour Prime Minister leading a fashionable society life met with intense disapproval from his supporters. In modern times, prime ministers have not tended to mix with London society, as it existed in pre-1939 days, or even with such remnants of it which have remained since 1945. Lloyd George, Bonar Law, Baldwin and Neville Chamberlain either did not have the time or the inclination to move in fashionable circles. Asquith was dragged into society by his wife Margot, not apparently very willingly but with no great reluctance. Sir Alec Douglas-Home led the life of a country gentleman. Attlee, Harold Wilson and Edward Heath never showed the slightest interest in social life (apart from relaxation) outside politics. Harold Macmillan enjoyed belonging to smart male clubs, such as Bucks and Pratts. Sir Winston Churchill was a law unto himself and, after he became Prime Minister in 1940, did not so much move among fashionable and aristocratic people as create his own personal court in which such people could certainly be found.

Since MacDonald's social life has contributed so largely to the mythology which surrounds the beliefs of those who subscribe to the dogma of 'The Great Betrayal', this life-style demands, in so far as it can be given, an explanation.

Despite a handsome and aristocratic appearance, a beautiful voice, fastidious taste, and a well-read and well-equipped mind, there is no evidence to support the belief, which is still held by some, that he was the illegitimate son of a Scottish nobleman. MacDonald was certainly illegitimate. His mother was a Miss Annie Ramsay, a servant girl in a farmhouse near Lossiemouth. Though she never married, she was the known and acknowledged mother of Ramsay MacDonald, with whom her grandchildren would spend their summer holidays. His father is thought to have been a ploughman named MacDonald, to whom Annie Ramsay became engaged and by whom she was made pregnant. They quarrelled, so the story goes, and never married. The future Prime Minister was christened James and later bore his mother's surname Ramsay and his father's surname MacDonald. He married a middle-class woman, Margaret Gladstone, a distant relative of the Prime Minister of that name. Her death in 1911 when he was only forty-five was, for him, an irreplaceable loss.

Then came the war years, and the ostracism which his opposition to the war engendered, and finally in 1918 the loss of his parliamentary seat. He appeared to be a ruined man. Yet four years later he was Leader of the Labour Party and little more than a year later became Prime Minister. The contrast between being lionised by every society hostess in London and being branded only a few years beforehand as a traitor was, perhaps, a little too sudden.

He was a lonely man who is known to have had only one affair after the death of his wife. The majority of his parliamentary colleagues were of inferior intellectual standard, and became increasingly uncongenial. There is no doubt that he found in society salons a social rehabilitation from the humiliations which he had endured because of his pacifist beliefs during the war and a substitute for the female companionship of which he had been starved since the death of his wife. So he frittered away night after night attending glittering social functions for the benefit of his solitude and his vanity, but to the detriment of his work.

A detailed analysis of Ramsay MacDonald's position, character and behaviour, as seen by third parties, has been necessary because he is the person, the only person in the context of the National government, against whom the accusation of betrayal has been levied. The other characters can be dealt with more speedily.

On the Labour side, the figures of fundamental importance were

Philip Snowden, Chancellor of the Exchequer in both Labour govern-
ments, and Arthur Henderson, the General Secretary of the Labour
Party, Home Secretary in the Labour government of 1924 and Foreign
Secretary in the Labour government of 1929-31. There were, it is true,
two other members of the so-called big five in the Parliamentary
Labour Party – J.R. Clynes and J.H. Thomas.

Clynes was in fact the Leader of the Labour Party in 1922 when he
was defeated by the newly re-elected Ramsay MacDonald when Parliament assembled after the general election of October 1922. At this
election the Labour Party had emerged as the second-largest party in
Parliament, and Ramsay MacDonald had been elected Labour Leader
by a mere two-vote majority. Clynes served with good grace under
MacDonald as Deputy Leader, as Lord Privy Seal and Leader of the
House of Commons in 1924, and as Home Secretary from 1929 to
1931. He served his Leader with commendable loyalty, largely owing
to instinctive loyalty to the labour movement as a whole. Clynes was a
poor Leader of the House of Commons and an undistinguished Home
Secretary. Nothing which he wrote in his two volumes of memoirs
shows that he possessed a glimmering of understanding of the issues
facing his country and government in 1931, and his conduct was
entirely consistent with his unquestioning loyalty to the Labour Party.

J.H. Thomas was a flamboyant character with a certain native
cunning which had ripened through his experience of many years of
negotiations with employers as General Secretary of the Railwaymen's
Union. He liked many of the good things of life, in particular drink,
cigars and good food. He relished his reputation as being a 'card'. He
deliberately dropped his 'aitches' and was frequently seen in white tie
and tails. He cited his telling of dirty stories to his monarch as evidence
of a comradely friendship, when it was more probably an example of
kingly forbearance and restraint. He was puffed up when the going was
good and collapsed when it was bad. He was ludicrously miscast by
MacDonald in the second Labour government as Lord Privy Seal in
charge of unemployment. He would greet Mosley, his junior Minister,
in the mornings with, 'Oh Tom I've an 'ell of an 'ead. I'll agree with
anything 'Orace [Sir Horace Wilson] says.' Beatrice Webb's assessment
of him was: 'Jimmy is a boozer, his language is foul. He is a stock exchange gambler, he is also a social climber. He is in fact our Birkenhead.'

This description was grotesquely and primly unfair to Lord Birkenhead, but Thomas came to grief in 1936 when he made Stock Exchange profits and leaked budget secrets to a friend. Not surprisingly, he followed MacDonald into the National government and remained a Cabinet Minister under Baldwin until his disgrace in 1936.

Philip Snowden was an altogether more formidable person. A cripple from youth, and a puritan by choice, he was by conviction a Gladstonian Liberal rather than a socialist. He had a fine brain and clarity of exposition. His intellectual talent, however, was marred by a rigidly narrow outlook. For him, free trade was a religion, a balanced budget was an article of faith, deficit financing was as immoral as drinking (he was a teetotaller) or adultery. MacDonald's indifference, Snowden's militant defence of the gold standard, and J.H. Thomas's bouts of lachrymose and alcoholic self-pity defeated Mosley's plans for alleviating unemployment from 1929 to 1930. Snowden was the perfect instrument to be used by the orthodox international bankers. He relished the ignorance of his Cabinet colleagues and appeared to take delight in imposing harsh and almost unbearable cuts in unemployment benefits to satisfy conventional financiers' requirements. Lord Davidson described Snowden in his papers:

> Snowden had an intellectual superiority, he was really a very remarkable man and I always liked him. Not everybody did and, of course, there were times when he let himself go and could 'take the skin off' his colleagues, for he could be a bitter man. That was the result of the fact that he was constantly in pain ... Snowden was so immensely gifted when compared to his Socialist colleagues and he came from a very much better background. Some people said he was very narrow, or, to put it differently, it was true to say that he knew, instinctively, that it was no good growing barley on deep clay soil. He knew that the Labour Party was useless when it was talking about finance.

It was not unfair to say that Snowden exploited its ignorance to the full in what seemed to him to be the not ignoble role of attempting to save the pound sterling in August and September 1931.

Arthur Henderson, the second most powerful man in the Labour

Party after Ramsay MacDonald, was unique in having been the only Labour Leader to have been in Lloyd George's War Cabinet (at which time he was actually Leader of the Labour Party in Parliament). He was therefore the only member of the 1924 Labour Cabinet who had previously held Cabinet office (with the exception of Lord Haldane, who was Lord Chancellor but had never formally joined the Labour Party). He had been a constituency Party Agent, and was General Secretary of the Labour Party and Foreign Secretary in the second Labour government. Henderson had strong ties with the trade union movement and consistently maintained that any Labour government must 'take the Trade Union Movement with us'. He had, in any event, resigned from the War Cabinet in 1917 to turn the Labour Party into a national movement, stating at the time that never again would he join a government in which Labour did not predominate. He was hardly suitable material for a Conservative-dominated National government, and he and MacDonald were bitterly antagonistic towards each other.

Stanley Baldwin was the principal figure on the Conservative side. He had already been Prime Minister twice, first in 1923, only six years after he had originally achieved junior Ministerial office, and second from 1924 until 1929. As with all ex-Conservative prime ministers who lose general elections, the Conservative instinct for cannibalism was directed against him and his leadership. In this matter, as in others, Sir Winston Churchill was an exception, although his ultimate retirement at the age of 80, while still Prime Minister, was enforced. Unlike Balfour, Sir Alec Douglas-Home and Edward Heath, who were victims, Baldwin managed, only just, to survive. He was first attacked by all those Conservatives, at that time nearly 100 per cent of the party, who believed that they had a divine right to rule. He was also assailed by a large body of opinion among rank and file Conservatives, who were under-represented in Parliament, who felt that his bipartisan approach on India, which was to culminate in the 1935 India Act, was tantamount to giving the Empire away. Baldwin was also attacked, as Balfour had been and as Edward Heath was to be, for failing to bring the Labour government down, by not opposing it strongly enough.

Such criticisms, which Conservatives always make of their leader when their party is in opposition, involve a certain degree of mathematical ignorance, or at least inaccuracy. A party is in opposition because it lacks the parliamentary support to form a government. In the twentieth century a government composed of one party has never fallen because its parliamentary supporters have withdrawn their support. Perhaps the reputation of Parliament would be enhanced if they were to do this, at least occasionally. But we must deal with things as they are and not as we might like them to be. A Conservative opposition cannot bring down a Labour government unless it can command more parliamentary votes than the government on a motion of no confidence, and if it can do this it is most unlikely to be in opposition.

In 1924 a wholly exceptional situation existed in which the Liberal Party in Parliament, although smaller than either the Conservatives or the Socialists, held 158 seats. By joining with the Conservative Party the Liberals were able to bring down the first Labour government in October 1924, having put Labour into power only nine months earlier.

Although Stanley Baldwin appeared to be a simple man, who smoked a pipe, loved rural life, and held conventional, though moderate, conservative views, he was in fact nothing of the sort. Outwardly conventional, he possessed some of the contradictions of personality which many people claim are to be found among the Celts. Indeed he was partly Celtic by ancestry. No simple man could have outwitted Lloyd George, Churchill, Beaverbrook, Rothermere, Birkenhead and Curzon as Baldwin was able to do. Though he was fond of country life and his native Worcestershire, his fortune derived from industry and not from land. It was, indeed, his knowledge of industry and the high standards which he set for himself as an employer that gave him a sympathetic insight into the mind of the industrial worker which none of his Conservative predecessors or successors have possessed, apart from Harold Macmillan. His outward appearance of indolence was sometimes misleading. He was at times indolent, and for the most part cautious, but he was capable of acting with great ruthlessness and speed as his subsequent conduct of the abdication crisis was to show. He was greatly admired by those of his political opponents in Parliament who came from the working classes. They knew that he was not one of the hard-faced men who had done well out of the war. They knew what he had tried to keep secret, that he had donated a fifth of his fortune (£120,000) to the Exchequer as a thanks offering for the country's survival of the war. They remembered his speech, possibly his greatest in Parliament, in 1926 in the famous Macquisten debate which ended with the words 'Give peace in our time O Lord'. He was praying for industrial peace. There was a simplicity of style and beauty of cadence in all his speeches, whether political or not, which is more common in poetry than prose.

Although a man of moderation, with views which were more often enlightened than conservative, Baldwin was not by nature a coalitionist, except in the sense that he believed that there were, and ought to be, many strands of thought within legitimate Conservative philosophy. His was the speech which carried the day so decisively at the Carlton Club meeting in October 1922, when he spoke in favour of the Conservative Party withdrawing from the Coalition government of which Lloyd George was the Prime Minister. As he was to say many times on the day before the National government was formed, 'Having destroyed one coalition I do not wish to form another.' His closest confidant from 1923 until 1937 was J.C.C. Davidson (later Lord Davidson) whose diary is frequently referred to in this book.

By the summer of 1931 Neville Chamberlain was already, through the strange customary processes then prevailing which provided for the emergence of a Conservative Party Leader, the acknowledged successor to Baldwin. His two most likely rivals had obligingly removed themselves from the scene. One, Sir Douglas Hogg, had become Lord Chancellor in 1928 and, as the first Viscount Hailsham, he never contemplated doing what his son was many years later lawfully enabled to do, namely disclaim his peerage.

Churchill, the other possible contender, was a much less certain starter. He had, in fact, resigned from what would now be called the Shadow Cabinet because he differed from his leader and other colleagues over their policy towards India. Even if he had not taken this step, many, including the author, doubt whether Churchill could ever in the first instance have become Conservative Leader and Prime Minister except in times of war. He had too many enemies in his own party, which he had left in 1905 and only recently rejoined. He was regarded by many as an unprincipled opportunist, prone to reckless misjudgements and none too fastidious in his choice of friends. His critics could build up a formidable case against him on these grounds in 1931.

Neville Chamberlain had only entered Parliament in 1918. Between

October 1922 and January 1924 he had become in quick succession Postmaster General, Minister of Health and Chancellor of the Exchequer. At the end of 1924 he returned to the Ministry of Health and in this post he left behind a legacy of social legislation which has probably never been equalled by any later Cabinet Minister. He founded the Conservative Research Department and therefore became, in opposition, the chief policy-maker of the Conservative Party. For a brief period he was the Chairman of the party organisation. He held this post when Conservative discontent with Baldwin had reached its height. Some people, including the author, believe that Chamberlain's loyalty to his Leader was less than wholehearted at this time. He appears to have been speedily forgiven by Baldwin for any possible lapse of loyalty in the preceding year; since August 1931 Baldwin deputed him to conduct virtually all the negotiations with Ramsay MacDonald which led, ultimately, to the formation of the National government.

Neville Chamberlain did not inspire affection in his political colleagues, although, until he became Prime Minister in 1937, he commanded almost universal respect. Even as Prime Minister he was greatly admired by the overwhelming majority of Conservative MPs who supported his foreign policy of appeasement. Despite his progressive social record he was greatly disliked by most Labour members of Parliament. Unlike Baldwin, he despised his intellectual inferiors and never attempted to make allowances for, let alone help to remedy, Labour's inexperience in office. He gave the impression of being less sympathetic, more narrow and more partisan than Baldwin. Oddly enough, though more partisan than Baldwin, Chamberlain was, as we shall see, much more in favour of a National government. When the crisis came, his first instinct was that the Labour government should be forced to take the unpopular decisions that he believed were necessary if the crisis were to be overcome. He said that the Labour government ought to do this in the national interest, although the electoral benefits that would accrue to the Conservative Party if this happened cannot have been excluded from his mind. When it became clear that the Labour government would not so act, he regarded a National government including Labour members, and preferably with Ramsay MacDonald as Prime Minister, as the next best alternative. Apart from the King, Neville Chamberlain exerted more pressure on MacDonald to lead a National government than any other leading participant in the events which unfolded.

Sir Samuel Hoare played a role in these events which was subordinate to that of Neville Chamberlain. He was a younger man – thirteen years younger than Baldwin and eleven years younger than Chamberlain. He was not a senior member of the previous Conservative Cabinet; indeed he had only held one Ministerial post, albeit for a considerable time. He was Secretary of State for Air from 1922 to January 1924 and from November 1924 to 1929. He was, probably, chosen by Neville Chamberlain to accompany him because, apart from Neville's half-brother Austen, he was, though younger, closer to him than any other colleague. Certainly when Neville Chamberlain was Prime Minister from 1937 to 1940 Hoare was his most intimate Cabinet colleague. He was an ambitious man (Lord Davidson subsequently commented, 'Sam Hoare was also a man of unlimited personal ambition') and was to become a successful Secretary of State for India from 1931 to 1935. His brief period as Foreign Secretary culminated in his resignation when the terms of the Hoare Laval pact were revealed. He was quickly restored to favour by Baldwin and was briefly First Lord of the Admiralty until he became Home Secretary in Neville Chamberlain's Cabinet in 1937. Had there been no war he would probably have succeeded Neville Chamberlain as Prime Minister. There is no evidence that Hoare and Neville Chamberlain at any time disagreed during the numerous, complicated and protracted series of meetings which they held with MacDonald and his colleagues.

Sir Herbert Samuel was, apart from Ramsay MacDonald himself, the most enigmatic figure in all that took place in August 1931. In many ways he had the most difficult role. He was the acting Leader, not the Leader, of the Liberal Party, the smallest party in Parliament. Despite a massive Liberal vote in 1929 which under a system of proportional representation would have secured nearly two hundred parliamentary seats, only 59 Liberal MPs were returned to Westminster. The Liberal Party had suffered from internal feuds since 1916. These feuds and the bitterness which they engendered almost certainly contributed towards the decline in the strength of the Liberal Party and the growth of the Labour Party. When Lloyd George supplanted Asquith as Prime

Minister in 1916 almost all the leading Liberals, including Samuel, who was the Home Secretary, declined to serve under Lloyd George. They in fact went on to perform the functions of a parliamentary opposition. When Lloyd George decided to hold an election at the end of 1918 those Liberals who had supported Asquith rather than himself did not receive the endorsement from him as Prime Minister and Bonar Law as Leader of the Conservative Party. This endorsement ('the coupon' as it was called) was given to 159 Liberal candidates and to all the 410 Conservative candidates. These Liberals, who were termed Coalition Liberals, were not opposed by Conservatives. In the resulting general election, 339 Conservatives and 136 Coalition Liberals were returned. The Independent Liberals were annihilated. Every single former Minister, including Asquith and Samuel, lost their seats and only 26 Liberals were returned. When Baldwin decided to hold a general election in 1923 on the issue of protection, the two parts of the Liberal Party came together with Asquith as Leader and Lloyd George as Deputy Leader. The short Parliament of 1924 revealed the astonishing sight of the smallest parliamentary party, the Liberal Party, with two former Prime Ministers as Leader and Deputy respectively and only 156 followers. Asquith was defeated for Parliament again in October 1924. He led the Liberal Party from the House of Lords until 1926 and died in 1928.

In 1929 Lloyd George found himself the Leader of a Liberal Party of only 59 MPs, many of whom, including Sir Herbert Samuel, had lost their seats eleven years earlier owing to his direct intervention. By 1931 a group of over thirty of these Liberals was already detaching itself from the Liberal Party under the leadership of Sir John Simon, who had also been one of Asquith's Ministers. Simon had evidently decided, together with his followers, to make himself stage by stage less distinguishable from a Conservative until there was no actual difference at all. However, in order to avoid the inconvenience of having to fight by-elections, they were 'converted' by slither rather than through battles on the hustings. Samuel, therefore, found himself as the deputy to a Leader for whom he can have had little love and the spokesman of a party which, thanks to the conduct of Sir John Simon and his associates, he could not control. Samuel had only returned to Parliament in 1929 after an absence of eleven years. For five years he had governed

Palestine as High Commissioner. His appointment had been greatly criticised by pro-Arabists, since he was a Jew. Nevertheless he had discharged his duties with distinction.

Of Samuel, it must ·be said that he was widely regarded by his contemporaries both inside and outside his party as not being entirely straightforward. This feeling could only have been increased by the subsequent publication of his memoirs. These contain too many apparent errors of fact to be accidental. In some cases, the errors of fact can be determined because they differ from every other available contemporary source. The memoirs of both Snowden and Samuel are so written as to present their conduct in the most favourable possible light. This is, of course, a very human temptation no doubt, indulged in to a greater or lesser extent by all who write autobiographies. In these two cases, however, the reader is left with the impression that, with the benefit of hindsight, *ex post facto* judgements have from time to time been imposed.

Samuel was a man of considerable intellect and of clarity of thought. As we shall see he, more than any other person, was responsible for convincing King George V of the desirability of a National government. (The author is not suggesting that Samuel acted at any time in bad faith or against the interests of his country or his party.)

Such were the personalities and records of the men who, unknown to them on 1 August 1931, were to be so dramatically involved in the historic events which culminated in the formation of the National government twenty-three days later.

2 PRELUDE

On 31 July 1931 the committee under the chairmanship of Sir George May, and commonly called the May Committee, issued its report. The creation of this committee stemmed from a Conservative vote of censure on the government's wasteful expenditure, especially in borrowing to meet the needs of the Unemployment Fund. This vote of censure was moved on 11 February 1931. A Liberal amendment to the Conservative motion of censure was tabled and this called for a special committee to review expenditure and recommend economies. Snowden accepted this proposal and appointed a committee with Sir George May, a former Secretary of the Prudential Assurance Company, as its Chairman. Four of its members were leading capitalists and two were trade unionists. No doubt Snowden hoped that the committee would advocate remedies which would force his Labour colleagues to accept the need for economy and persuade the Conservative Party to accept increased taxation. It must again be stressed that for Philip Snowden a balanced budget was an article of faith.

From the standpoint of Britain's national interests, the May Report could hardly have been published at a more unfortunate time or in a more damaging way. Parliament had risen that day; on the previous day there had been a debate on the economy. Snowden, of course, knew the contents of the May Report, though he only referred to them in the most general terms in his speech. This was sombre in tone but Snowden restricted himself to saying that the House must unite and balance the budget. Neville Chamberlain had seen Snowden before the debate on 30 July and knew of the contents of the May Report; it was agreed between them that all-party co-operation would be necessary in what was diagnosed by the May Committee as being a major economic crisis. In the debate, therefore, Chamberlain restricted himself to an appeal to Snowden to be 'true to England and not to shut one's eyes to unpleasant facts'.

The May Report predicted that by April 1932 the budget deficit would reach £120 million. The majority of its members (the two trade

unionists dissenting) argued that it was essential to balance the budget
in order to preserve and restore international financial confidence in
Britain. They therefore recommended new taxation amounting to £24
million a year and a reduction in expenditure of £96 million. Two-
thirds of the recommended cuts were to be provided by cutting unemployment benefit by 20 per cent and there were to be 10 per cent
cuts in civil servants' salaries and in the pay of teachers, servicemen
and the police. The report was published without any government
comment and the government attached so little urgency to it that,
although before Ministers dispersed for their holidays an Economic
Committee of the Cabinet was set up consisting of MacDonald,
Snowden, J.H. Thomas, Arthur Henderson and W. Graham, it was not
due to have its first meeting until 25 August. Although nobody was to
know this at the time, the date chosen was to prove to be the day after
the National government was formed. The report was on the whole well
received by the Press, although Keynes called it 'the most foolish document I ever had the misfortune to read'. Keynes went on to argue that
the May Report 'invites us to decide whether it is our intention to make
deflation effective by transmitting the reduction of international prices
to British salaries and wages' or, as he proposed, 'so long as the slump
lasts to suspend the sinking fund, continue borrowing for unemployment insurance and impose a tariff'. W. Ashworth, the economic historian, said of the May Report many years later:

> The report presented an over-drawn picture of the existing financial
> position; its diagnosis of the causes underlying it was inaccurate; and
> many of its proposals (including the biggest of them) were not only
> harsh but were likely to make the economic situation worse, not
> better.

A.J.P. Taylor wrote in his book *English History 1914-1945*,

> The May report treated the sinking fund of £50 million a year (that
> is the repayment of debt) as an untouchable charge of revenue;
> insisted that all unemployment relief must be paid out of income;
> and thus arrived at an immediate deficit of £120 million or £170
> million in a full year. The five rich men on the Committee

recommended, not surprisingly, that only £24 million of this deficit should be met by increased taxation and £96 million by economies, two thirds at the expense of the unemployed whose relief should be cut by 20% . . . Snowden and the Treasury had their ammunition for a stern budget.

At this point it must be said that the Bank of England, the joint-stock banks, the City and the Conservative and Liberal parties all accepted the validity of the conclusions of the May Report. Indeed the Bank of England view as expressed by Sir Ernest Harvey, the Deputy Governor (Sir Montagu Norman, the Governor, was ill throughout the crisis), and Edward Peacock, a Director, to Ramsay MacDonald in the middle of August 1931 was:

(1) that we were on the edge of a precipice and unless the situation changed rapidly we should be over it directly: (2) *that the cause of the trouble was not financial but political and lay in the complete want of confidence in His Majesty's Government existing among foreigners;* and (3) that the remedy was in the hands of the Government alone.

MacDonald and Snowden became convinced that both the diagnosis and the remedy were correct. No single member of the Labour Cabinet questioned the diagnosis or the remedy. Eleven out of 21 members of the Labour Cabinet were reluctantly, and as a last resort, prepared to back proposals broadly similar to those proposed by the May Committee. The minority of nine in the Labour Cabinet, whose threatened resignation made the continuation of the Labour government impossible, did not suggest an alternative remedy. They simply wanted a Tory or at least a non-Labour government to do what they shirked doing themselves.

It was left to Keynes and certain other economists, the General Council of the TUC led by Ernest Bevin (who was heavily influenced by Keynes), and Sir Oswald Mosley, who had left the Labour Party, to reject totally the bankers' view, to maintain that the existing currency system based on the gold standard had broken down, that the financial crisis of 1931 was a key symptom of this breakdown and that the bankers' advice, which was aimed at restoring the free working of the system, offered no solution at all. Not one member of the Labour Cabinet suggested or even believed that the gold standard could or should be suspended; yet this act was taken by the National government on 21 September 1931, less than one month after its creation, even though the main purpose of its creation was to avert this disaster. Sidney Webb (Lord Passfield), one of the Labour Ministers who resigned, subsequently complained: 'Nobody told us we could do this.'

At this point it is probably convenient to nail the allegations that the majority of the previous Labour Cabinet was in favour of introducing a tariff against manufactured and semi-manufactured goods entering Britain. Such a decision, taken purely on its merits, would have ended the Liberal support for the government and enforced its resignation. It is necessary to make this clear because during the general election of October 1931, Snowden, who was still Chancellor of the Exchequer, though now in the National government, chose to reveal that two votes had been taken by the Labour Cabinet in August 1931. He alleged that a vote was taken on a proposal to impose a 10 per cent tax on manufactured and semi-manufactured products, and stated that fifteen members of the previous Cabinet had voted in favour of this proposal and five against. Snowden also stated that the question of a duty on all imports, including food and raw materials, was put to the vote and that five voted in favour of this proposal and fifteen against. It is most unusual for a Cabinet Minister to reveal what occurred in a previous Cabinet of which he was a member only a few months before, but Snowden was not the only culpable person. Former members of the Labour Cabinet who refused to serve in the National government (or were not asked to serve), and some of those who did serve in the National government, on occasions quite shamelessly broke the convention of Cabinet confidentiality in the House of Commons, in speeches outside the House of Commons, in the Press and on the radio. The bitterness between these two groups had reached such a level that these lapses of behaviour were probably inevitable. In fairness, however, to all concerned, the proposal for a revenue tariff appears to have come from J.H. Thomas, who was both in the Labour Cabinet and in the National government. The position of those members of the Labour

Cabinet who voted in favour of tariffs and the context in which they did so was put by Mr Arthur Henderson in a speech at Accrington on 19 October 1931, during the general election campaign.

> He [Snowden] knows quite well that there was only one reason why we ever gave any consideration to a revenue tariff. It was because of his determination to balance the budget by cutting down unemployment benefits and social services and our desire to find some alternative.
>
> There was never any question of a majority of my colleagues committing themselves to the principle of tariffs. It was simply a question of the lesser of two evils. Faced with the impossible proposition of refusing out-of-work benefits, a revenue tariff seemed to some of us a less disagreeable alternative.

In August 1931 Neville Chamberlain was, perhaps, more committed than anyone to introducing tariffs, but he wanted this in addition to cuts in unemployment benefits — not as a substitute. As Chancellor of the Exchequer in the National government (the post he assumed in succession to Snowden after the general election of 1931), he was to bring in a revenue tariff in 1932 and, although he encountered no opposition from the Conservative Party or from Simonite Liberals, who had become in effect Conservatives under another name, his action led to the resignation of Snowden and the Liberals from the National government. This makes it very clear that the Labour Cabinet, in August 1931, could only have accepted tariffs if they were prepared to sacrifice the Liberal support which for two years had given them their majority in Parliament.

To return to the narrative, between 31 July, when Parliament had adjourned and the Prime Minister, Ministers and party leaders had dispersed for their holidays, and the second week in August, there had been a serious run on the pound. Foreigners were selling their sterling at a great rate. The original reasons for this were somewhat technical and had little to do with the budget deficit or even Britain's deficit in her balance of payments. It has been suggested by many economists that the origin of the monetary crisis may have been the revelation by the German Foreign Minister, on 19 March 1931, that there was to be a customs union between Germany and Austria. This move was strongly opposed by France, and within two months, on 11 May 1931, Austria's largest bank, the Credit-Austalt, had declared itself bankrupt, largely because of French speculation. The French tried to prevent a standstill of the bank's creditors but this was nevertheless achieved by the end of May. A foreign loan to the Austrian government was then negotiated, but at the last minute the French, who were expected to take up a substantial part of the loan, made their participation conditional on the abandonment of the customs union. Sir Montagu Norman therefore decided to provide the entire loan. In the meantime there had been a run on the Reichsbank of Germany. Montagu Norman was therefore approached by Herr Luther, the President of the Reichsbank, for a credit from the Bank of England and the Federal Reserve Bank. The latter made French participation a condition of their own. The French not only put economic pressure on Germany but withdrew large sums in gold from London, spreading the rumour that Britain's budget for 1931-2 would not balance and that Britain would have to seek a loan from France. In fact the Bank of England had been borrowing from French depositors at 2 per cent and lending to Germans at 8 per cent. The German banks were forced to repudiate their liabilities by declaring a moratorium. The London bankers then revealed that they owed foreign depositors £250 million. They had borrowed short-term and lent long-term.

The run on the pound could only have been stopped by control of the international exchanges and the blocking of foreign funds, but this was incompatible with the maintenance of the gold standard. By 22 July 1931 the Bank of England had lost £22 million in gold. It lost £33 million in gold and a further £33 million in foreign exchange during the next fortnight. On 1 August it was announced that the Bank of England had obtained £25 million credits from France and New York. On 4 August Sir Ernest Harvey, Deputy Governor of the Bank of England, deputising for Sir Montagu Norman, who was ill, withdrew the Bank's support of sterling, doubtless hoping that the gold losses would jolt the government into action over expenditure cuts. On 5 August the Bank lost £4.5 million in one day, and Harvey had to report that £66 million in gold and foreign exchange had been lost in a fortnight. Further loans had to be sought from France and the United

States. These countries insisted that some dramatic act was necessary for international confidence in the pound to be restored. That act had to be a balanced budget. It was to find a means of achieving this dramatic act that was the purpose of the innumerable meetings of the Economic Committee of the Cabinet, meetings of the Cabinet itself, and meetings between politicians of all parties, and between politicians and bankers and the TUC.

For four further days the pressure on the pound continued. Snowden therefore telephoned MacDonald in Scotland, who returned to London on the night of 10 August. In the meantime Harvey asked Snowden if he might contact the leaders of the Opposition. Neville Chamberlain returned to London on 13 August, Sir Herbert Samuel, the acting Liberal Leader, returned to London on the night of 12 August, and Stanley Baldwin, after some show of reluctance, arrived in London on the morning of 13 August.

It is now necessary to give, as far as possible, a day by day account of all the meetings which took place, and to record as accurately as possible what each of the persons most intimately involved said or did.

On Tuesday 11 August 1931, the Prime Minister and Snowden saw Sir Ernest Harvey and Edward Peacock. The Prime Minister had earlier in the morning of the same day seen Sir Clive Wigram, the King's Private Secretary. From 11 a.m. until 5 p.m. the Prime Minister and the Chancellor of the Exchequer were in conference with Harvey and Peacock, and according to Snowden were in consultation with 'a number of representative bankers', who included Reginald MacKenna, a former Chancellor of the Exchequer and currently Chairman of the Midland Bank.

The collective advice given to the Prime Minister and the Chancellor by the bankers was that the credits from the United States and France were rapidly disappearing and that there was no chance of a further loan from either. The bankers also warned MacDonald and Snowden that the government itself would have to borrow £80 million since the credit of the Bank of England was being so rapidly exhausted. MacDonald's diary quotes the bankers as saying, 'The failure to balance Budget is forfeiting confidence in sterling: something should be done at once to prove that Budget is to be balanced.' The bankers then proceeded to give the Prime Minister and Chancellor the warning which has already been referred to earlier in this chapter, and which was mentioned in a letter written by Neville Chamberlain to Sir Philip Cunliffe-Lister, then a Member of the Conservative Shadow Cabinet, on 15 August 1931. Chamberlain went on to write in the same letter:

> As they [i.e. the bankers] were still in serious doubt as to whether any action would be taken, they asked to be allowed to put the facts before other parties. R.M. assented and it was in response to a message from the Deputy Governor that I went to London.

After the conference with Bank of England officials on 11 August, MacDonald called a meeting of the Cabinet Economic Committee for 4 p.m. on Wednesday 12 August, to be resumed on the morning of Thursday 13 August, and again on Monday 17 August.

MacDonald has been criticised by some members of the Labour Cabinet who resigned on 24 August, and by many members of the Labour Party then and since, for giving the bankers permission to put the facts before the leaders of the other parties. He was also criticised at the time, and since, for holding a series of meetings with Conservative and Liberal leaders between sessions of his own Cabinet. What his critics do not allow for is that his government was in a minority in the House of Commons. In 1929, 288 Labour MPs had been returned as against 260 Conservatives and 59 Liberals. The Labour government therefore at its inception could have been defeated in the House of Commons by a combined Conservative and Liberal majority of 31 votes.

Since 1929, several by-elections had been won by the Opposition parties. MacDonald's Labour government could therefore at any time have been overthrown by a combination of its opponents. It was necessary for him to be able to carry the bulk of the Liberal Party with him in any emergency legislative measures (hence the delicacy of the tariff issue), and with the likelihood of a revolt from his extreme left wing some Conservative votes might well have also been needed. At the very least he needed to know whether decisions made by his Cabinet would carry any support outside the Labour Party, for if this were not the case his only alternatives would have been to resign or to call a general election. If, like Attlee in the 1945-50 period, MacDonald had possessed a parliamentary majority of nearly 200 over all other parties, inter-party consultation would not have been necessary, although, at a time which nobody disputes was one of national crisis, it would not have been unusual and might even have been advisable. Certainly these meetings in themselves, which were held with the full knowledge and consent of his colleagues in the Labour Cabinet, provide no evidence that MacDonald was conspiring with the Opposition leaders behind the backs of his own colleagues. Indeed they bear some similarity to the meetings which were held between James Callaghan and David Steel and between Labour Ministers and Liberal parliamentary spokesmen in 1977.

3   12 AUGUST

At 4 p.m. on Wednesday 12 August the Economic Committee of the Cabinet met. The official records of the Cabinet meetings are now available. The Cabinet Economic Committee meetings were not minuted. There are, of course, the memoirs of some individual members of both bodies, and two further documents. These documents represent the recollections of the former Labour Ministers who did not join the National government of what transpired at these meetings. In the case of the proceedings of the Cabinet Economic Committee, the dissenting Ministers were Arthur Henderson, the Foreign Secretary, and William Graham, then President of the Board of Trade. This document is commonly referred to as the Graham Memorandum, since it was drafted by William Graham. The other document, which was approved by all the former members of the Labour Cabinet (except MacDonald, Snowden, Thomas and Lord Sankey, who were members of the National government), was drafted by Arthur Greenwood, who had been Minister of Health, and relates to the proceedings which took place in full Cabinet meetings. The author will call this document the Greenwood Memorandum.

The Graham Memorandum states that at the first meeting of the Cabinet Committee on 12 August two of its members (presumably Henderson and Graham) were 'somewhat surprised' to learn that the Prime Minister and the Chancellor had already been in 'informal conversations' with the Opposition leaders. In fact, however, none of the Opposition leaders had arrived in London by then. Samuel was due to arrive later that night and Baldwin and Chamberlain did not reach London until the following day. It is clearly doubtful whether any direct conversations had yet taken place: nor had the Opposition leaders come to London at the Prime Minister's request as suggested. The Graham Memorandum is clearly incorrect on this point.

It was, in fact, the bankers who asked the Prime Minister for permission to put the facts before the leaders of other parties when they met MacDonald and Snowden on 11 August. This permission was granted by MacDonald. Sir Herbert Samuel, the acting Liberal Leader, stated in his memoirs that while staying in Norfolk he received a telegram asking him to come to the Bank of England on a matter of importance. Neville Chamberlain wrote: 'It was in response to a message from the Deputy Governor that I went to London.' Baldwin wrote to Davidson, his close confidant, from Le Havre on 12 August: 'I have been summoned back to meet Neville and Horne [Sir Robert Horne, a former Conservative Chancellor of the Exchequer], which Geoffrey Fry says is urgent.' He added that he hoped to return to France the following night. From this letter it seems most improbable that he though that he would even be meeting the Prime Minister.

It is important that these movements should be stated in detail, because both the Graham Memorandum and the Greenwood Memorandum on more than one occasion make surmises and carry innuendoes which are simply not borne out by the facts. The duty of a historian is never to contravene the facts when they are known, to put forward all the facts that are available, and then to draw from these facts such conclusions as appear to him fair and reasonable.

At the first meeting of the Cabinet Economic Committee its members were informed by Snowden that the estimated deficit for the financial year 1932-3 was £170 million and not the May Committee's figure of £120 million. The Committee had, when it first met, a set of proposals drawn up by the Treasury. These proposals were in line with the recommendations of the May Committee that the budget must be balanced, but instead of achieving this result by economy cuts accounting for three-quarters of the gap and extra taxation only one-quarter, the Treasury plan provided that approximately as much would be raised by fresh taxation as was to be saved by economies. In particular the Treasury proposals only suggested a 10 per cent cut in unemployment benefit as compared with the 20 per cent demanded by the May Committee. It is not clear how much ground had been covered at this first meeting of the Economic Committee, since there is no official record of its proceedings, but arrangements were made for it to meet again on Thursday 13 August at 11 a.m.

4 13 AUGUST

The first meeting which MacDonald and Snowden held with an Opposition Leader was with Sir Herbert Samuel. This meeting was held before the scheduled meeting of the Economic Committee for 11 a.m. This is clear from the newspapers of the following day, although Samuel in his memoirs states, inaccurately, that he was seen after Baldwin and Chamberlain, who were not in fact seen by the Prime Minister and Snowden until 2 p.m., as all other available accounts confirm. Samuel wrote in his memoirs of his meeting that he was told 'the Budget deficit for the current year would be £40 million, and was estimated for the next year at no less than £170 million'. He went on:

> The Government and its advisers were agreed that drastic economies in expenditure, and equally drastic increases in taxation were indispensable, only in that way would the Budget be balanced. And only if it were balanced could confidence in the £ sterling be restored and the crisis overcome. The Minister communicated to us the measures they proposed to their colleagues.

It is somewhat doubtful if this last statement is accurate; there was no reason to believe at this stage that the Cabinet Economic Committee had agreed to recommend any proposals to the Cabinet as a whole, indeed the reverse was almost certainly the case, since MacDonald's diary makes it clear that there were strong disagreements among the members of the Cabinet Economic Committee on 17 and 18 August, several days later.

Chamberlain's account of the meeting which he and Baldwin had with MacDonald and Snowden at 2 p.m. on 13 August sounds more plausible. He wrote to Sir Philip Cunliffe-Lister:

> At the interview R.M. was characteristically vague and woolly, but as I knew what I wanted to know, I was able to put one or two questions which elicited definite answers from him or Snowden, and the

position now is pretty plain. I summarise it briefly. The Cabinet Committee have decided that the Budget must be balanced, but that there must be equality of sacrifice. The May Committee contains many impossible recommendations, but the Departments concerned are to be told to make their own proposals for reduction . . . the total reduction aimed at being in the neighbourhood of £100 millions. This will leave a large gap to be made up out of taxation. I don't know what it is, but the Chancellor said the situation was worse than indicated by the May Committee.

According to Chamberlain, Baldwin 'asked no intelligent question, made no helpful suggestion', but this may well have been due to his anxiety 'to be gone' before he was 'drawn into something'. Certainly Baldwin did not wish to be drawn into a coalition with Labour, for which Chamberlain was already 'showing enthusiasm'.

Davidson in his draft memoirs summed up Baldwin's attitude after he and Chamberlain had met MacDonald and Snowden as follows:

S.B., although at the time quite unwilling to envisage coalition, went out of his way to indicate that the Conservative Party would take a helpful line in Parliament; but he said that he could not promise full co-operation until the exact nature of the Government's proposals were known. After the meeting was over, he decided that he would resume his holiday while Neville Chamberlain remained in London.

Neville Chamberlain was delighted at Baldwin's departure, since it gave him a much freer hand in his negotiations with MacDonald and Snowden. He wrote to his sister on 16 August:

Anyway the decisions are left to me as S.B. is not coming back. I think he would agree that crises of this kind are not his forte. He left a final message for me that he was most grateful to me for sparing him the necessity of returning and he would 'back me to the end!' So I go back tomorrow night. I have asked Sam Hoare to come and attend the Conference with me.

Characteristically Baldwin left the scene only to re-emerge some 36 hours before the National government was formed. Any suggestion, and it has many times been suggested, that MacDonald as Leader of the Labour Party and Baldwin as Leader of the Conservative Party conspired together to form the National government can thus almost certainly be disposed of.

By the evening of Thursday 13 August the Economic Committee of the Cabinet had met twice and was due to meet for a third time on Monday 17 August. This was to be a critical meeting because the Economic Committee would have to make positive recommendations to a full meeting of the Cabinet which MacDonald had called for Wednesday 19 August. Samuel, Baldwin and Chamberlain, representing the Liberal and Conservative parties, had had one meeting with the bankers and one with the Prime Minister and the Chancellor. There had as yet been no tripartite meeting involving the Labour, Conservative and Liberal Party leaders. On the evening of Thursday 13 August MacDonald and Chamberlain both left for Scotland. Baldwin had already departed for Aix-les-Bains. Although Middlemas and Barnes have stated in *Baldwin – a Biography* that a three-party meeting had been fixed for 3 p.m. on Tuesday 18 August, which Baldwin asked Chamberlain to handle, this meeting did not in fact take place. MacDonald's diary for 17 August states:

Chancellor has found week-end all too brief for preparations & I found a letter from him saying he would not be able to meet Liberals & Tories tomorrow as arranged, so I sent messages to Chamberlain, Snowden and Maclean accordingly.

A meeting which had, in fact, been planned in advance on 13 August was a joint session between the Cabinet Economic Committee, the TUC General Council and the Labour Party National Executive. This was fixed for Thursday 20 August at 3 p.m.

5   17, 18 and 19 AUGUST

The Economic Committee of the Cabinet met duly on Monday 17 August and a further long meeting was held on Tuesday 18 August. It will be recalled that the Economic Committee was due to put forward proposals to the Cabinet at a full meeting which was to be held at 11 a.m. on Wednesday 19 August. By that time the Economic Committee had met on four occasions. The Treasury plan which was tabled for its consideration had already been outlined. It is known that the committee started its proceedings by examining the various economy measures which had been put forward by the Treasury. This was revealed later by Arthur Henderson in a speech made to the House of Commons on 8 September 1931. In this speech Henderson claimed that he had wished the committee first to consider ways of raising additional revenue. Nobody has disputed Henderson's claim, which is confirmed in MacDonald's diary, but it evidently did not achieve the support of the majority of the members of the committee, since the committee started by considering expenditure cuts.

MacDonald's diary for 17 August states: 'We dispersed at 10 o'clock having ticked down expenditure provisionally by £87m p.a.' It is important at this point to make it clear (because no member of the Cabinet Economic Committee ever sought to assert otherwise) that the committee did not come to the Cabinet with any definite recommendations, indeed the word 'provisionally' quoted from MacDonald's diary is significant. Henderson and Graham, as Ministers who subsequently resigned, have insisted upon this point, and Snowden, who remained as Chancellor of the Exchequer in the National government, described the results of the committee's deliberations as 'only tentative proposals for consideration'. They appeared before the Cabinet on one piece of paper without any comment, and are contained in Appendix V, p. 134.

On the other hand to argue, as the ex-Ministers afterwards did, that the tentative nature of the proposals permitted any member of the Economic Committee subsequently to reject them all cannot be admitted, for as R. Bassett, in his book *Nineteen Thirty One: Political Crisis*, so clearly put it, 'the obvious answer was that such action rendered the whole process of considering and submitting economy proposals a sheer waste of time, unless, indeed, those concerned were prepared to propose alternative economies.' This they showed no inclination to do.

It is also important to recognise that two highly controversial measures, one to reduce expenditure and the other to increase revenue, did not form a part of these 'tentative proposals for consideration'. The May Committee had proposed a 20 per cent cut in the standard rate of unemployment insurance benefit, although the Treasury suggestions had reduced this figure to 10 per cent. The Economic Committee did not put forward any proposals for a cut in the standard rates, but only in the transitional benefits. The question of a revenue tariff was certainly discussed by the Economic Committee as an alternative to a cut in the rates of unemployment benefit. All members of the Economic Committee, with the exception of J.H. Thomas, were against the principle of a revenue tariff, but all except Snowden preferred this to a cut in unemployment benefits, and there was, according to MacDonald's diary, a vote of '4 in favour and the Chancellor against'. Henderson and Graham claimed that they had said that if one of the two alternatives had to be adopted they could not in any circumstances agree to a cut in the standard rate of unemployment insurance benefits. This did not of course mean that the controversial items could not be discussed in full Cabinet. Indeed both were discussed and voted upon by the members of the Cabinet.

The list of economies submitted to the Cabinet at 11 a.m. on Wednesday 19 August totalled £78,575,000 and were as follows:

Unemployment insurance	£43,500,000
Teachers' salaries	11,400,000
Service pay	9,000,000
Police pay	500,000
Roads	7,800,000
Other economies	6,375,000

The figure of £43.5 million in respect of unemployment was divided into two parts. There were to be increases in contributions by employers and workers and there was to be a reduction of the Treasury contribution to transitional benefit. The standard rate of benefit, however, was to remain unaltered.

When they met at 11 a.m. on Wednesday 19 August the members of the Cabinet had not collectively sat together since Parliament rose at the end of July. The Cabinet sat for nearly nine hours with short intervals for luncheon and dinner. It rose at 10.25 p.m. After all this discussion, the Cabinet had reached no definite conclusions on the economic package. Some progress had been made. Provisional agreement had been reached on economies totalling £56,250,000 and this figure included £25.5 million relating to unemployment insurance. The proposal to save £20 million on the Exchequer contribution towards transitional benefit, which had been included in the global figure of £43.5 million in respect of unemployment, was referred to a subcommittee of four: Arthur Greenwood (Minister of Health), Graham (President of the Board of Trade), Tom Johnston (Lord Privy Seal) and Miss Margaret Bondfield (Minister of Labour). The fact that the Cabinet had not reached anything approaching a final decision was particularly worrying in view of the forthcoming three-party conference which had been authorised by the Cabinet and was due to take place at 10 a.m. the next morning. This was to be followed at 11 a.m. by a meeting between the Cabinet Economic Committee and the Consultative Committee of the Parliamentary Labour Party, a meeting which had been called at the insistence of Arthur Henderson. There was also to be, at 3 p.m. on Thursday 20 August, a joint meeting of the Cabinet Economic Committee, and the TUC General Council and the Labour Party National Executive, which Snowden had only agreed to attend under protest.

The absence of any announcement after a Cabinet meeting of such length did not go unnoticed by the Press. *The Times* described it as 'disquieting' and the *Daily Express* referred to a 'Cabinet All-day Tariff Battle'. It was thought that a vote had been taken at the Cabinet Meeting on 19 August on a revenue tariff on manufactured goods and that fifteen members had voted in favour and only five, including Snowden, against, but this is not recorded in the Cabinet minutes. MacDonald's private diary for 19 August states: 'I asked opinions on Revenue Tax. 15 for. 10 on manufactured goods only. 5 on everything.'

The Cabinet minutes disclose that a final decision was deferred until 21 August. It is probable that Snowden, alone, would at this point have brought his opposition to a revenue tariff to the point of resignation. This is perhaps the clearest evidence of the dominance wielded by Snowden over all his colleagues on fiscal matters.

6 THURSDAY 20 AUGUST

The three-party conference, which the Cabinet had authorised the Prime Minister to convene, took place at 10 Downing Street at 10 a.m. on Thursday 20 August. The Conservatives were represented by Neville Chamberlain and Sir Samuel Hoare, the Liberals by Sir Herbert Samuel and Sir Donald Maclean, and the government by the Prime Minister and Snowden. Hoare refers to the presence of J.H. Thomas but this, though quite possibly accurate, has not been confirmed elsewhere.

The Opposition leaders were told for the first time that the estimated deficit was £170 million (Samuel claims in his memoirs to have been given this figure on 13 August, but he had probably mistaken the date since he would hardly have been given information that had been denied to Chamberlain or to members of the Cabinet). Again Samuel has created some confusion as to what occurred at this three-party conference on 20 August, since in a speech on 14 September 1931 he stated: 'We were told that the Cabinet Committee had met and had prepared certain proposals which it was intended to lay before the Cabinet but they had not then been considered by the Cabinet.' However, everybody knew that the Cabinet had met for nine hours on the previous day, and it must have been inconceivable to anybody that the proposals had not been considered by the Cabinet, which of course they had. By contrast, Neville Chamberlain recalled that Snowden put forward economies of some £78 million. Chamberlain declared that the cuts were inadequate and

> stressed two points, first that in view of the increased estimate of the deficit, to produce economies less than the aggregate recommended by May (£96 million) was wrong and second, that if unemployment benefit were left untouched, the contemplated economies . . . would certainly be jeopardised. In effect, the Prime Minister and Snowden gave us to understand that they quite agreed, the latter saying that if you took into account both the fall in the cost of living and the rise in the benefits, the unemployed were 36% better

off than in 1924.

In making this remark Snowden had, perhaps, overlooked the fact that the number of unemployed in 1924 was just over a million and by August 1931 very nearly three million.

Some people, most notably C.L. Mowat, author of *Britain between the Wars*, have criticised Snowden and MacDonald for putting forward the figure of £78 million for economies to the three-party conference and 'not the £56 million provisionally accepted the previous evening'. In fairness to both it must be pointed out that the £56.25 million accepted by the Cabinet on the previous evening represented a partial acceptance of the Economic Committee's proposals, and indeed a working party had been set up to consider and report back on a further £20 million. It would be quite contrary to the doctrine of collective Cabinet responsibility for Snowden to have reported other than he did, unless the Cabinet had actually rejected the further economies, which by appointing the working party it obviously had not done. Sir Samuel Hoare, writing of this meeting, says: 'Snowden was obviously speaking to a Cabinet brief, and made no effort to conceal his personal opinion that it did not go far enough.' Here, possibly, Snowden acted imprudently. The Opposition leaders left to consult their colleagues.

A brief meeting between the Cabinet Economic Committee and the Consultative Committee of the Labour Party took place at 11 a.m. at Downing Street. Seven members, including Chuter Ede, were present. They were received by the Prime Minister, Henderson, Graham and Thomas. Since the meeting with the Opposition leaders was still in progress elsewhere in No. 10, the Prime Minister left almost at once, returning at 11.30. Chuter Ede

gathered that the Conservative and Liberal Parties insisted on the cost-of-living cut in unemployment benefit. The seven members of the Consultative Committee had a brief discussion after the meeting, and according to Ede unanimously decided that if the Government accepted the terms of the Opposition Parties 'it was very doubtful if they would get any other votes from our party other than the lawyers'.

The presence of J.H. Thomas at this meeting at No. 10 provides a plausible explanation for the assertion of Hoare that he was also present at the meeting with the Opposition leaders, since he may well have attended a part of both.

The most significant meeting of the day (20 August) and possibly of the entire crisis was that held between the TUC General Council, the Labour Party National Executive and the Cabinet Economic Committee. It was held in the Council Chamber of Transport House at 3 p.m. It brought about a sharp difference of opinion which was shortly to become a final breach between Snowden and Henderson, the two most powerful men in the Labour Party apart from the Prime Minister himself, and both possessing support from the grass roots of the Labour Party which MacDonald had allowed to wither. Henderson had been a lifelong trade unionist, and had also, as its Secretary, created the Labour Party organisation. To him it seemed not merely natural but essential that the government should consult with the trade union movement as well as the Opposition parties and the Bank of England. Snowden had not entered Parliament through the trade union movement; he regarded a meeting between members of the Cabinet and the TUC General Council as almost unconstitutional. He attended the meeting with reluctance, spoke unwillingly and imparted to the TUC General Council less information than he had given to the Opposition leaders earlier that day. He had stated before the meeting that he had never recognised the right of the TUC to be consulted over Cabinet policy. In view of Snowden's attitude and subsequent accusations made by the Conservatives, Snowden, and supporters of MacDonald that the TUC had attempted to 'dictate' to the government, it must be stated that the TUC did not demand a meeting with the Cabinet. On the contrary the invitation to a joint meeting came from the Cabinet itself. No trade union leader at the time made any claim that the government was in any way bound to consult the TUC. There was clearly no constitutional impropriety in the decision of the Cabinet to seek the views of the TUC General Council. Nor was there any constitutional impropriety in the Cabinet or the Prime Minister consulting the bankers, or the Opposition party leaders.

It so happens that the TUC General Council, largely influenced by Ernest Bevin, the General Secretary of the Transport and General

Workers' Union, diagnosed an ailment and prescribed a remedy which
was dramatically different from those diagnosed and prescribed by the
bankers and Opposition leaders. As Bevin, according to Alan Bullock,
remarked later: 'If the General Council had supported the Prime Minister, they would have been hailed as "statesmen"; when they disagreed
they were accused of dictation and invading the privileges of the
Cabinet.' They were soon to find themselves attacked for anti-patriotic
as well as unconstitutional action.

In fact, however, the TUC made no industrial threats of any kind; it
did make a strong plea for a further meeting with the Prime Minister
and the Cabinet Economic Committee and at this meeting put forward
its own proposals for solving the crisis which, though strikingly different
in character, were no more dictatorial (indeed they were less so) than
those put to the Prime Minister and Snowden by the Deputy Governor
of the Bank of England, Sir Ernest Harvey, and Edward Peacock on 11
August. In fairness to these two gentlemen, however, it must be stated
that they first put a leading question to the Chancellor before giving
their advice. Lord Citrine (the plain Walter Citrine), at that time
General Secretary of the TUC, writes in his memoirs:

> I was asked whether I would meet privately some of the bankers
> who had been discussing the situation with the Government. I at
> once consented, and one evening in the Travellers Club in Pall Mall I
> met Edward Peacock (later Sir Edward Peacock) and one of his
> fellow directors of the Bank of England. Peacock showed himself
> very sensitive to the charges which were being made against the
> bankers, and he repeatedly stated that the Bank of England (which
> was not then nationalised) had not attempted in any way to influence
> the Government's policy. They had seen the Chancellor of the
> Exchequer, Philip Snowden, privately and had asked him the straight-
> forward question: 'Does the Government wish to remain on the
> Gold Standard? If so, certain steps must be taken to secure econo-
> mies in public expenditure. If you do not want to stay on the Gold
> Standard, tell us now, and we shall know what to do.' Snowden
> had replied without any hesitation and, apparently without consul-
> ting anyone at that stage, that of course we must stay on the Gold
> Standard. Peacock told me that he was informed later that Snowden

had notified Ramsay MacDonald of his answer and that Ramsay fully agreed with him.

Nobody, of course, has suggested that there was any impropriety in bankers and trade union officials having consultations with each other on this matter.

The meeting between the Cabinet Economic Committee, the TUC General Council and the National Executive of the Labour Party was unproductive. It lasted for only an hour. Walter Citrine made a very detailed report on 7 September 1931 to the Trade Union Congress about Snowden's statement at the joint meeting, which R. Bassett in *Nineteen Thirty One: Political Crisis* has summarised as follows:

(1) The Cabinet Committee had been considering a series of proposals; they had not accepted any of them: none were final, none definite.

(2) The practice of providing unemployment benefit by borrowing could no longer be continued: the deficit on the Insurance Fund, and the amounts necessary for transitional benefits would have to be met out of revenue.

(3) It was proposed to increase contributions by £15 million, £5 million each from the workers, the employers and the State; and to reduce to 26 weeks the period of insurance benefit.

(4) These are the only two proposals we are making. There is no proposal for a cut in the amount of unemployment benefit.

(5) Reductions would have to be made in the salaries of certain classes of public and Government employees (Snowden specified teachers' salaries; the pay of servicemen and police; the salaries of Cabinet Ministers, Judges etc.).

(6) There would be a reduction of approximately £8 million on roads.

(7) Only approximately half the deficit would be covered by the proposed reductions, and consequently there would have to be increased taxation based on the principle of equality of sacrifice. Snowden steadfastly refused to disclose the methods of raising the additional revenue.

It was this refusal on the part of Snowden to state how he intended to apply the principle of equality of sacrifice that led to the angry termination of the meeting at 4 p.m.

Much was made subsequently of different interpretations which were placed upon paragraph (4) of Bassett's summary. The Greenwood Memorandum states that the Chancellor said 'that a cut in Unemployment Benefit was not a part of the Government's proposals'. Snowden in his *Autobiography* wrote: 'I put before the meeting a statement of economies on which the Cabinet had already agreed, but pointed out that at the present they had not decided upon a reduction in the unemployment allowances. That statement however was not my intention.' Bassett reproduced on page 92 of his book *Nineteen Thirty-One: Political Crisis* what purports to be a shorthand note made by Citrine himself which substantiates Snowden's version as to what he said, although Citrine, according to Bassett, had no recollection of making the shorthand note. In his own autobiography *Men and Work*, which was published after the death of Bassett, Citrine appears to bear out Snowden's explanation, although it was Citrine himself who in September 1931 had originally challenged it. The only conclusion that can be drawn from a difference of interpretation placed upon one sentence which became a major issue in the general election of 1931 is that there was a genuine conflict of opinion between Snowden and his opponents as to what he meant in that sentence, which was open to ambiguity in any circumstances, and all the more so in the atmosphere of that particular meeting.

It had been agreed by the TUC that Arthur Hayday, the Chairman, and Walter Citrine, the General Secretary, would be the sole spokesmen for the General Council at the joint meeting, but Ernest Bevin, undoubtedly the most formidable of the trade union leaders, protested at the way in which MacDonald had dramatised the situation. The Prime Minister had, said Bevin, given interviews of the most dramatic character to the *Daily Mail* and he complained that the *Manchester Guardian* and *The Times* had been more fully informed than the party's own newspaper and Bevin's child, the *Daily Herald*. The Prime Minister invited the TUC representatives to meet the Cabinet Economic Committee again and they did so at 9.30 p.m. that evening when they put forward their own proposals. In the meantime the TUC General

Council deliberated for four hours before deciding that it must oppose all the Cabinet proposals. The key figure in the discussions was Ernest Bevin.

Bevin was born in 1881, the son of an unmarried mother. He was educated at an elementary school. In 1910 he became the leader of the Dockers' Union. He created the Transport and General Workers' Union and was its General Secretary from 1921 until 1940, when he entered Churchill's wartime government as Minister of Labour and National Service. He and MacDonald had disliked each other for a long time, but this had not stopped them from working together. MacDonald had offered Bevin a peerage, which was refused, and had appointed him a member of the Economic Advisory Council. By far the most educative experience in financial matters for Bevin had been his appointment as a member of the Committee on Finance and Industry which had been set up in 1929 under the Chairmanship of Lord Macmillan. In the first place he came into close contact with J.M. Keynes, who was also a member. He also, with his quick native intelligence, gained a detailed knowledge of the workings of finance. He was the only trade union member of the committee, which contained four bankers, including Reginald MacKenna, Chairman of the Midland Bank and a former Liberal Chancellor of the Exchequer, and R.H. (later Lord) Brand, managing director of Lazards. Fifty-seven witnesses appeared before the committee, including the Governor and Deputy Governor of the Bank of England, the Chairman of the joint-stock banks, Sir Richard Hopkins, Secretary to the Treasury, a distinguished group of economists, and numerous representatives of commerce and industry.

In the words of Alan Bullock, his biographer:

In Bevin's view, instead of monetary policy being guided by the needs of industry and trade, the Bank and the Treasury attached far too much importance to the maintenance of the pound's exchange rate, to the prestige of London as the centre of the International Money Market and to the 'sacred cow' of the gold standard, leaving Industry to bear the consequences in the shape of falling prices, wage cuts and unemployment.

It is hardly surprising that, holding such views, he gave an unsympa-
thetic hearing to MacDonald and Snowden at the meeting on 20 August.

On 17 August 1931 Bevin had given his own diagnosis of the crisis
to the Executive of his union:

> The crisis has not arisen as the result of anything that the Labour
> Government has done, or of the social policy of the country or even
> the cost of unemployment. It has arisen as a result of the manipula-
> tion of finance by the City, borrowing money from abroad on what
> is termed a 'short term' or 'ready cash' basis and lending it on long
> term, causing several of the big financial houses in London to
> wobble almost to the verge of bankruptcy, due to the fact that they
> could not realise on the loans made and thus meet the calls from
> those from whom they had borrowed. As usual the financiers have
> rushed to the Government, but they have put up a very good smoke
> screen, attributing the blame for the trouble to the social policy of
> the country and to the fact that the budget is not balanced. There-
> fore the City must be saved at the expense of the working class and
> the poorest of our people.

When the trade union representatives returned to 10 Downing Street at
9.30 p.m. on Thursday 20 August, they rejected totally the suggested
government measures and put forward four alternative proposals.
These were:

(1) replacement of the unemployment insurance scheme by a grad-
    uated levy upon the whole community, based on the capacity
    to pay;
(2) the suspension of the Sinking Fund for the National Debt, the
    annual contribution to which amounted to £50 million;
(3) new taxation upon all fixed-interest-bearing securities;
(4) a revenue tax (which was left open).

Harold Nicolson in his life of King George V describes MacDonald as
having returned to 10 Downing Street after the joint meeting with the
TUC General Council in a mood of furious despair. He can seldom have
lived through a more cruel day. He and Snowden had been told by

Neville Chamberlain at the three-party meeting at 10 a.m. that economies of £78.5 million were not enough; Snowden had at least convinced Sir Samuel Hoare that he privately agreed with Chamberlain's views; MacDonald knew that his Cabinet had in fact only accepted a figure of £56.25 million (although a working party was looking at a possible extra £20 million); the total rejection of any economies by the trade union leaders in Nicolson's words 'aroused his personal vindictiveness and steeled his resolve'.

A short Cabinet meeting was held at 8.30 p.m. when members were told of the reaction of Chamberlain to the economy measures and of the rejection of any economy measures by the TUC.

The Prime Minister and Snowden, according to the Cabinet minutes, informed the Cabinet that the Conservative leaders had expressed doubts about the contemplated cuts in the fighting services and felt that the unemployment insurance cuts did not go far enough. They did not raise the question of a revenue tariff. The Prime Minister said that he had had a second meeting with Neville Chamberlain who wanted economies of approximately £100 million.

Graham, the President of the Board of Trade, is reported in the Cabinet minutes as saying that he had held a second meeting with Sir Herbert Samuel (MacDonald's private diary reveals that Samuel and Graham had dined with him just prior to the Cabinet meeting), who had been in touch with Mr Lloyd George, the Leader of the Liberal Party. The Liberals, too, favoured more drastic cuts in unemployment insurance benefits but, significantly, they had declared themselves to be most strongly opposed to a revenue tariff in any shape or form. Since the Labour government depended upon the support of over fifty Liberals for their parliamentary majority this total rejection of a revenue tariff on their part inevitably made this no longer a viable alternative to unemployment insurance benefit cuts.

Henderson, the Foreign Secretary, is somewhat surprisingly recorded in the minutes as saying that the Consultative Committee had adopted a very reasonable attitude and that it had, in effect, adjourned until the eve of the re-assembly of Parliament. Henderson's report of the committee's attitude is in direct conflict with that of Chuter Ede. Since, however, Ede's record was made public some time after the formation of the National government he may, like so many of the characters in this drama, have been speaking with the benefit of hindsight, and when the Labour reaction to MacDonald was at its most hostile peak. It was also reported to the Cabinet that the National Executive, which Henderson had insisted should be consulted, had agreed to leave the whole question to the government.

The Cabinet Working Party on Unemployment Insurance in its report recommended a slight rearrangement of contributions, saving only £4 million and not the £20 million required. The Chancellor stated that this fell far short of what was needed. The Cabinet adjourned until the following morning so that the Economic Committee could meet the trade union leaders at 9.30 p.m.

The trade union proposals were put forward by Bevin and Citrine. Snowden was the only Minister to speak from the government side, except MacDonald who summed up at 10.30 p.m., saying that nothing the General Council representatives had put forward touched the actual problem that faced the government. Henderson said nothing at this meeting, but there is no doubt that his views had been greatly influenced by the two meetings with the TUC General Council (its earlier one including the National Executive) held that day. Henderson was no expert in financial matters, and if the General Council of the TUC had accepted the full economy measures he would almost certainly have done the same, in which case there would have been few, if any, Cabinet resignations and possibly no National government. He was far from happy with the cuts, but until Ernest Bevin had put the case with forceful clarity Henderson was apparently unaware that a respectable and even convincing case could be advanced in which the whole economic strategy of the government and the banks could be challenged.

MacDonald's diary for 20 August[1] makes clear the bitterness which he felt at Henderson's support of the TUC view and of the union representatives themselves. MacDonald wrote that 'they undoubtedly voice the feeling of the mass of workers. They do not know and their minds are rigid and think of superficial appearances and so grasping at the shadow lose the bone.'

The TUC case, which was virtually Bevin's was that the cause of the crisis was not in Britain but in Germany. Financial houses in London had made loans to German institutions which could not be repaid at short notice. These funds had been borrowed from France and America where nervousness was shown about the state of British credit, hence the serious withdrawal of funds from London. The British banks, the government and finally the Press took up the cry and alleged that the economic position was so alarming that foreign confidence must be restored by dramatic economies. A budget deficit, so the TUC argument went, was irrelevant, since all the leading industrial countries were running budget deficits. (Certainly the balanced emergency budget which was to be introduced by Snowden in September did not stop the flight from the pound, which was devalued by the National government on 21 September.) What was needed, said the TUC, was expenditure in modernising industry, international action to raise the world level of wholesale prices, devaluation of the pound and an investigation into the possibility of a revenue tariff. The National government was forced into devaluation, unwillingly, less than a month later and, after shedding Snowden and the Samuelite Liberals, embraced tariff reform twelve months later. The TUC policy was not necessarily the answer to the government's problems but it could be argued on respectable intellectual terms, as one would expect from its principal originators, Bevin and Keynes.

Note

1. MacDonald wrote, 'Henderson never showed his vanity and ignorance more plainly.'

7 FRIDAY 21 AUGUST

On Friday 21 August the Cabinet had yet another meeting lasting for more than five hours. Harold Nicolson states that its members agreed that 'no Government worthy of its name could for one instant submit to dictation from an outside body such as the T.U.C.' There is no evidence that this was said in the Cabinet. Indeed the Cabinet minute states 'The Chancellor of the Exchequer reported that the meeting had been a friendly one.' In the Cabinet minute Snowden goes on to say that the TUC General Council was wholly opposed to all the economies except for the reduction in the salaries of Ministers and judges. Snowden is also quoted as saying that the TUC had pressed for the largest possible extension of a public works policy provided that the works themselves were of an economic character. The Cabinet minute, which bears no trace of resentment, ends: 'It was agreed that it would be necessary to inform the General Council that the Government regretted that there was no alternative to their programme.'

Sidney Webb, however, said to his wife: 'The General Council are pigs, they won't agree to any "cuts" of Unemployment benefits, or salaries or wages.' Nevertheless, by now, Henderson[1] and probably at least half the members of the Cabinet recognised that the TUC was advocating a serious economic alternative to the government policies, even if it had not fully been formulated. As David Marquand has written in his book *Ramsay MacDonald*:

> The unemployed had been victimised already by being thrown out of work: to victimise them all over again, in order to find a way out of a crisis which was none of their making, would be to make a mockery of everything the Labour Party stood for.

What happened at the Cabinet meeting on 21 August was a reaffirmation of the Cabinet's acceptance of economies of up to £56,400,000 (Appendix VI, p. 136), thus substantially strengthening their provisional acceptance of approximately £56.25 million on 19 August. The ques-

tion of a revenue tariff was raised for the final time and, in the words
of the Cabinet minute, 'It was represented that since the last discussion
of this question by the Cabinet the situation had been altered by reason
of the rejection by the Liberal Party of any such expedient.' The Prime
Minister closed the subject by confirming that there would be no decision in favour of a tariff. No further progress was however made on the
extra £20 million. In her diary for 22 August, Beatrice Webb wrote:

> Parliament is to be summoned on September 14th: the Government
> expects to be defeated and the Conservatives will take office. 'No
> resignations' urged Ramsay MacDonald and 'no general election until
> the budget is balanced' . . . The bankers have let us in for it by their
> £150 million long-term credit to Germany, whilst accepting short
> term deposits of £200 million from other Countries. The German
> Credit cannot be withdrawn, whilst the other Countries are with-
> drawing their deposits because British finance is not solvent: And
> the British people are not solvent because of the dole: He [Sidney
> Webb] thinks J.R.M. has behaved in all good faith over the whole
> business.

For some extraordinary reason the Cabinet dispersed for the weekend
on Friday 21 August with economies amounting to only £56,400,000
agreed among them in the full knowledge that MacDonald and Snowden
were to meet the Opposition leaders again at 5 p.m. that evening, and
that the Opposition leaders had been told that economies of £78
million were proposed which in their view were insufficient. In fact the
Cabinet had minuted that Ministers should arrange to be available in
case a further meeting of the Cabinet had to be summoned to deal with
any special emergency but, as will be seen, most of them left London
immediately after the meeting.

Earlier in the day, Neville Chamberlain had consulted those of his
colleagues who were still in London. Lord Davidson wrote in his draft
memoirs: 'These included Cunliffe-Lister, Hailsham, Eyres-Monsell,
Kingsley Wood and myself. They all agreed that the cuts that were
proposed would not effectively restore confidence abroad unless there
was also a cut in unemployment benefit.' Of course, Chamberlain was
talking of the £70 million mentioned by Snowden the previous day. Sir

Herbert Samuel and the Liberals expressed themselves rather more warmly in favour of the tentative proposals of £78 million of 20 August. In his speech to the House of Commons on 14 September 1931 Samuel said,

> We had consultations with our political friends and the Conservative party representatives had similar consultations, and we were all of the opinion that those proposals represented a very bold scheme, and a courageous attempt to grapple with the realities of the situation, but we doubted whether such a large sum of savings could be effected with regard to unemployment without a diminution in the scale of unemployment allowances, and we were determined to raise this point at the next conference. We were prepared to give a general assurance of support if measures of that kind were laid before Parliament.

When, however, the three-party conference met at 10 Downing Street at 5 p.m., the Prime Minister stated that the Cabinet had modified the Economic Committee's plan and 'has struck roughly one-third off the proposals'. Chamberlain in his diary (he wrongly states that the meeting took place at 3 p.m.) wrote: 'We asked whether it was proposed to announce that this was the last word, and were told "yes". When we asked what would happen if this announcement failed to restore confidence . . . Snowden replied "the deluge".' Hoare protested loudly and MacDonald asked, in what Chamberlain's diary calls a jocular way, 'Well, are you prepared to join the Board of Directors?' According to Iain Macleod, in his biography of Neville Chamberlain, Hoare said that 'if seriously meant, that was a proposition which would demand serious consideration'. Then, at Herbert Samuel's suggestion, the Conservatives and Liberals withdrew to consult among themselves and afterwards among their colleagues. At some time, therefore, after 5 p.m. on Friday 21 August Ramsay MacDonald, for the first time that can be authenticated, made a formal proposition to the accredited leaders of the Opposition parties that a National government might be formed.

The *Daily Herald* of 22 August reported that, to the surprise of the onlookers in Downing Street, members of the Cabinet began to arrive back before the Opposition leaders left. The *Herald* disclosed that 'an emergency Cabinet meeting has been called, but that owing to the short notice it had not been possible to get all the members together.' Those Cabinet Ministers who had arrived at No. 10 then left, and a special Cabinet was summoned for 9.30 a.m. on Saturday 22 August. The Opposition leaders returned to Downing Street at 9.30 p.m. According to Iain Macleod[2] and Middlemas and Barnes[3] they found MacDonald alone, but Sir Samuel Hoare refers to Snowden and Thomas being present, although at a later stage Hoare wrote: 'He [MacDonald] asked Chamberlain and me to talk to him alone in his upstairs sitting room.' It seems probable that Hoare was right and Macleod and Middlemas and Barnes were wrong and that after Snowden, Thomas and Samuel had left, he and Chamberlain remained behind for a private talk with MacDonald.

Of the meeting on the evening of 21 August Chamberlain wrote in his diary:

> I opened first and intimated (1) that if these were the final proposals
> . . . we should turn them out immediately the House met (2) that
> before then, we anticipated that the financial crash must come (3)
> that we considered that it was his the Prime Minister's bounden duty
> to avoid that crash and (4) that we were ready to give him any
> support in our power for that purpose either with his present or in a
> reconstructed Government. Samuel followed on exactly the same
> lines, not a word being said about a National Government though I
> think it was fairly clear that we were not excluding such an eventu-
> ality. In reply the P.M. began by drawing a touching picture of his
> own position (a thing he loves to do). He had founded, nursed,
> cherished, built up the Socialist Party. It was painful enough to leave
> an old Party: what must it be for him to contemplate killing his own
> child. He did not think resignation would help. He would remain
> P.M., assert his own views, invite his colleagues to support him and
> tell those who would not that they might go 'where they liked'.

Sir Samuel Hoare, the other Conservative present, wrote:

> Snowden supported by Thomas was obviously ready to accept
> Chamberlain's requirements. MacDonald, who certainly did not

disagree with his two colleagues, was nervous of undertaking the responsibility of a decision that at least half his Cabinet and all the T.U.C. opposed. Even when he implied at the last of the conferences that he was ready to break with the dissidents and carry on as best he could, it was clear to me that he felt that the task would be beyond his powers. His doubts became more evident when, after the last evening, he asked Chamberlain and me to talk to him alone in his upstairs sittingroom. It was late in the evening, and the room was almost dark when for many minutes he soliloquised to us about his own troubles and the country's need of an all-party effort. His words like the atmosphere, were obscure, but the conclusion that Chamberlain and I drew from them was the same. He had decided to resign, and to advise the King to send for the party leaders for consultations as to the next step. Having no instructions from Baldwin, we could give him no advice, least of all on the question of his own resignation.

According to Davidson, 'Chamberlain urged that he should consider the possibility of the formation of a National Government.' It had always been Chamberlain's reserve position that, if the Labour Cabinet would not carry through the economy measures in full, MacDonald should be detached, remaining as Prime Minister but splitting the Labour Party. In his private dairy, written on 22 August, MacDonald wrote of the meeting with Chamberlain, Hoare and Samuel. He stated that Chamberlain

> wished to add that if I wished to form a Government with their co-operation they were willing to serve under me. Sir H. Samuel concurred. I told them that I would take into account the 22nd and see them after Cabinet tomorrow.

It will be seen that there are discrepancies between MacDonald's diary and that of Neville Chamberlain. MacDonald ascribes words to Chamberlain which the latter specifically disclaimed. However the latter wrote 'not a word being said about a National Government, though I think it was fairly clear that we were not excluding such an eventuality'. It must be assumed from MacDonald's diary that the message had clearly been taken, although, as we shall see, the eventual answer was still far from certain.

Notes

1. An example of Henderson's somewhat confused mind can be given when he insisted, against all his Cabinet colleagues, that the Cabinet had agreed to an economy relating to the insurance premium which would have saved £2.5 million a year. Against his protests this economy was actually deleted by the Cabinet on 21 August.
2. Iain Macleod, *Neville Chamberlain* (London, 1961), p. 150.
3. Keith Middlemas and John Barnes, *Baldwin – A Biography* p. 623.

8 SATURDAY 22 AUGUST

Between the first and second of the three-party meetings which were held on 21 August, Neville Chamberlain had telephoned Baldwin at Aix-les-Bains telling him that it was imperative that he should return to London immediately. Baldwin left for Paris that night. Davidson met him in Paris the following morning, and Baldwin and Davidson reached Victoria Station at 7.30 p.m. on Saturday 22 August. From there they drove straight to Davidson's house in Great College Street.

The King had been at Sandringham since 11 August and it had already been announced that he would be leaving for Balmoral on the night of 21 August. He had in fact suggested to the Prime Minister that he might postpone his visit to Balmoral, but MacDonald persuaded him to keep to his original plans since if they were cancelled at the last moment this might give rise 'to alarming rumours and cause consternation'. The King therefore left for Balmoral, arriving there early in the morning of Saturday 22 August.

The Cabinet met at 9.30 a.m. on 22 August since, as we have seen, the attempt to recall it on the previous evening had been unsuccessful. The Prime Minister and Snowden reported on the attitude of the Opposition parties. There was at the time, for those who were not present, some confusion as to what they said. According to the Greenwood Memorandum:

> The Prime Minister and the Chancellor reported. A demand was made by the Opposition leaders for further economies amounting to £25 million to £30 million (in addition to the £56 million) the bulk of which was to be found out of Unemployment Insurance. Both the Prime Minister and the Chancellor made this statement.

An allegation to this effect was made by Arthur Henderson in his speech in the House of Commons on 8 September. But Neville Chamberlain said in the House of Commons at the conclusion of the economic debate on 14 September: 'there was no demand for a specific

increase in the economies. There never was a demand for a specific cut
in unemployment benefit.' This statement of Chamberlain's was not
strictly true, since what had occurred was that MacDonald and Snowden
told the Cabinet, according to the Cabinet minutes, that the Opposition
parties would not support the government in Parliament on the basis of
the existing £56,400,000 put forward and that support would not be
forthcoming unless the economies were raised by £25-30 million and
that the greater part of the increase must be found from a cut in
unemployment benefits. MacDonald and Snowden went on to say that
the Opposition leaders had suggested that unless this were done Parliament should be summoned without delay and the two parties would
combine to defeat the government. The Cabinet was also told that a
moratorium would probably be unavoidable by the following Wednesday
and that the government needed to negotiate credits of £80 million
immediately.[1] The Greenwood Memorandum stated that the Prime
Minister and Chancellor saw the bankers on the previous evening
between 7 p.m. and 9.30 p.m. during the adjournment of the three-
party conference when, no doubt, this advice was given. (MacDonald's
diary gives the time of the meeting as 4.15 p.m.) The Cabinet minutes
for 22 August confirm this. MacDonald and Snowden told the Cabinet
that it was impossible to wait for the re-assembly of Parliament and
that immediate decisions had to be taken to avoid the moratorium.
Henderson stated afterwards that he then said:

> 'Mr Prime Minister, I have had a growing conviction that we are
> being asked to handle a situation that it will be quite impossible for
> us to carry through . . .' I said 'That conviction is stronger now than
> it has ever been,' and I went on to say, 'and you can think of it what
> you like. The sooner the position is ended, the better so far as I am
> concerned.'[2]

The Cabinet minutes state that the Chancellor of the Exchequer said:

> So far as he was concerned he had no doubt whatever that, if he was
> compelled to choose between retaining the Labour Movement in its
> present form and reducing the standard of living of the workmen by
> 50% which would be the effect of departing from the Gold Standard,

he knew where his duty would lie.

Beatrice Webb in her diary of 23 August refers to the Cabinet meeting on the 22nd:

> Henderson blames the P.M. for spending so much time in negotiation: he thinks that it would have been far better to have settled really what the Labour Cabinet would be prepared to do in economies and resign if it were rejected by the Opposition, assuming that it was not possible to await the decision — owing to the action of the international financiers — of the House of Commons on September 14th.

She also wrote of the same meeting:

> J.R.M. raised the question of a Co-alition Government: some of the Labour Cabinet Ministers remaining in office. This he intimated was what the King desired and might propose. This proposal Henderson and other members hotly rejected. The impression left on S.W.'s mind was that J.R.M., Snowden and Jimmy MIGHT CONSIDER IT. 'A good riddance for the Labour Party' I said. They rose at 12 o'clock under the impression that the P.M. would resign and Baldwin would take office.

The Greenwood Memorandum, however, says that the question of a coalition or national government was raised by the Prime Minister but that Snowden expressed the view that the Cabinet would be unanimously opposed to the formation of such a government. There is no confirmation in the Cabinet minutes that MacDonald did, in fact, raise the question of the formation of a National government. There is a somewhat elliptical paragraph in the minutes which reads as follows: 'Arising out of the report made to the Cabinet summarised in the previous conclusions the Cabinet discussed at considerable length the procedure to be adopted in the immediate future in the event of certain contingencies arising.' It is reasonable to assume that, in the light of the entry in MacDonald's private diary as to the offer made to him the previous night by Neville Chamberlain, the Greenwood Memorandum was correct. If this is so, it must be emphasised, there was no question of MacDonald's going behind the backs of his colleagues, indeed he could hardly have been more frank.

The Greenwood Memorandum states that the Cabinet was faced by the Prime Minister with alternatives of a 10 per cent cut in unemployment benefit or the practical certainty of a moratorium on the following Wednesday. According to Harold Nicolson, Snowden then made a passionate appeal to his colleagues and in response:

> Grudgingly the Cabinet agreed to allow the Prime Minister to 'enquire' of the Opposition whether if the economy figures were raised from £56,375,000 to £76,000,000 including a 10% cut in unemployment relief, the Government could then count on Conservative and Liberal support. This suggestion was to be put to the Opposition solely and simply as an 'enquiry' and without in any way implying that the Cabinet as a whole had agreed to such increases.[3]

A substantially similar account is given in Snowden's autobiography.[4] The Greenwood Memorandum states:

> A vote was taken as to whether the Prime Minister should approach the Opposition leaders to enquire whether if the Cabinet agreed to include a 10% cut, plus £7 million other economies in their tentative proposals, this would obtain their support for the scheme as a whole. It was agreed that the Party leaders should be seen, the Cabinet not being committed to such a proposal.

These three accounts are broadly in agreement, and the terms of the enquiry to be made by the Prime Minister and the Chancellor are confirmed in the Cabinet minutes but they are, of course, totally contradicted by Beatrice Webb's statement that they rose at 12 noon under the impression that they would resign. Beatrice Webb also states in her diary: 'However in the luncheon hour J.R.M. and Snowden met the Opposition leaders again and suggested another compromise (S.W. said that J.R.M. was not authorised to do it).'[5] The Cabinet minutes state: 'The Cabinet decided to adjourn in order to enable the Prime Minister and the Chancellor of the Exchequer to confer with the Opposition party leaders and to re-assemble on the same day at 2.30 p.m. to receive a report from the Conference.' The entry referred to above is one of many extracts from Beatrice Webb's diary in August 1931 which casts the most serious doubts on its reliability and on the accuracy of Sidney Webb's recollections of events during this particular period. This unreliability is especially borne out by the fact that the Cabinet did not *rise* at 12 noon as Beatrice Webb claimed; it *adjourned* at 12.10 to enable MacDonald and Snowden to meet the opposition leaders and *resumed* its meeting at 2.30 p.m. to hear the results of the consultations, as the Cabinet minutes make plain beyond any doubt.

Although neither Keith Feiling, Chamberlain's official biographer,[6] nor Iain Macleod, the author of *Neville Chamberlain*,[7] mention this meeting in their works, a meeting was held at 10 Downing Street at 12.30 p.m., which was attended by MacDonald, Snowden, Neville Chamberlain, Sir Samuel Hoare, Sir Herbert Samuel and Sir Donald Maclean.[8] MacDonald said: 'When it was put to the representatives of the other political parties they said to us "Will this scheme secure the loan?" If it does we will support it. If it does not, we shall not.'[9] MacDonald is reported in the Cabinet minutes as saying,

Mr. Neville Chamberlain had made a reservation to the effect that the acceptance of the proposition by the Conservatives must not be taken as precluding the Conservative Party from pressing for further reductions on Unemployment Insurance when the legislation was before the House.

Snowden wrote:

We received the impression that if this could be done [i.e. secure the confidence of the bankers] they would regard the total of our economies as satisfactory. But they urged that this was a matter upon which the bankers should be consulted and, if they were satisfied, the Opposition leaders would raise no objection.

The Cabinet met again at 2.30 p.m. According to the Greenwood Memorandum:

The Prime Minister reported that the Opposition leaders would probably agree to this. It was then suggested that these suggestions should be placed before the Bankers. Though there was a division of opinion on this, it was decided to take the step. The Cabinet was not however to be committed to the 10% cut plus £7 million. The Bankers were to be told this and asked whether, if it *were* acceptable to the Government, it would satisfy New York.

At 3 p.m., according to the Cabinet minutes, the Prime Minister withdrew from the Cabinet meeting to see Sir Ernest Harvey and Edward Peacock. When he returned, the Cabinet minutes quote him as saying,

If the answer was favourable the Prime Minister proposed to see the Leaders of the Opposition Parties and to discuss with them the Parliamentary situation. If the answer were unfavourable it was not proposed to have any further meeting with the Party Leaders.

The minutes go on, 'The Cabinet agreed to the procedure suggested by the Prime Minister.' From this account it is clear that MacDonald was in no circumstances prepared to support economies beyond the 10 per cent cut plus £7 million. As MacDonald had already reported to the Cabinet that the Conservatives might, according to Neville Chamberlain, press for a still larger cut in unemployment insurance benefit, the only interpretation that can be placed on his final sentence is that he would resign together with the entire government if any further concessions were asked for either by the bankers or by the Opposition parties. MacDonald said, 'Again, with full consent, representatives of the Bank of England were consulted as to whether in their opinion the scheme proposed would produce the loan.'[10] Sir Ernest Harvey and Edward Peacock, when consulted, replied that they would immediately put the case to the New York bankers and obtain their opinion. The Federal Reserve Bank of New York was debarred by its charter from making loans to foreign governments, therefore negotiations had to be conducted through the British government's agents in New York, Messrs J.P. Morgan, with a consortium of New York bankers. Nevertheless, at the request of the Prime Minister, the Bank of England asked the President of the Federal Reserve Bank, George L. Harrison, for an advisory opinion. The Cabinet adjourned at 3.40 p.m. and it was agreed that it would meet again at 7 p.m. the following day (Sunday 23 August) to await a reply.

There is no record, nor any newspaper report, of anyone conferring with the Prime Minister at any time during the evening of 22 August. The *Sunday Times* of 23 August stated that the Chancellor of the Exchequer and Mrs Snowden left 11 Downing Street for their country home in Tilford, Surrey, shortly after the Cabinet meeting had ended. Mr Malcolm MacDonald has informed the author that his father telephoned his family at Lossiemouth on the evening of Saturday 22 August saying

> that he expected the Labour Cabinet to reject the policy which he thought they should adopt in the crisis, or at least that so large a minority would oppose it that the Government would not continue in office. He said that he would cease to be Prime Minister and so go on the Opposition benches in the House of Commons – although from that side of the House he would support the Conservative Government (which he expected to come into office with Liberal support) if it introduced the same economies in legislation as he had favoured in the Labour Cabinet.

The principal Conservative leaders spent the evening of 22 August at Davidson's house in Great College Street. In *Memoirs of a Conservative*, by Robert Rhodes James,[11] Davidson recollects the evening:

> We [Baldwin and himself] had dinner together at my house, and afterwards Neville Chamberlain and Hoare came into the Library. This was a very pleasant room and, most important, it fortunately was not overlooked at all from other houses so it was possible to have a completely private meeting.

Davidson's draft memoirs continue:

> Chamberlain and Hoare had seen MacDonald shortly after midday and were able to give S.B. an up to date account. The Cabinet had met that morning and MacDonald had told them of the views of the

Opposition. Apparently there had then been a rather ambling discussion in which Henderson had expressed the opinion that the Government ought to resign, and Thomas had raised the question of a National Government. Snowden had opposed this passionately and at the end, at his insistence the Cabinet agreed that he and MacDonald should find out from the Opposition leaders what their attitude would be to cuts totalling some £76 million which included a 10% cut in unemployment benefit.

This report is quoted in full, because it must have been most unusual, if not unique, for a Prime Minister to confide in a leading member of the main Opposition party (Chamberlain and Samuel were seen separately by MacDonald) to such an extent that he actually described a blow by blow account of a Cabinet disagreement, even going so far as to define the attitudes taken at the Cabinet by naming his principal lieutenants, and the roles which they played. It could be deduced from this that, by Saturday lunchtime, MacDonald was already starting to treat Chamberlain as a potential colleague and certainly not as a political opponent. This does not mean that MacDonald had by that time decided to form a National government, although on only the previous evening he had asked Chamberlain whether he was prepared to join the Board of Directors. It is probable, however, that Saturday's Cabinet meeting had undermined MacDonald's belief that the Labour government would continue to be able to govern, and this is fully borne out by Malcolm MacDonald's telephone conversation with his father mentioned above. In those circumstances, betrayed as he possibly felt by his own Cabinet and possibly, as he thought, about to become a back-bencher, he opened his heart to Chamberlain, who had every reason to be friendly and sympathetic because of the role that he had in mind for his confidant.

Davidson continued in his draft memoirs:

The discussions at my house that evening [22 August] were inconclusive. S.B. was deeply reluctant to envisage a new Coalition. He had destroyed one and did not wish to form another. Neville Chamberlain became very impatient with S.B.'s attitude. He made it quite clear that he could see no other way out of the situation; S.B.

agreed that if that was indeed the case it would be his duty to take part in it. It was clear, however, that he was still very worried about the whole idea.

In the meantime the King had arrived at Balmoral. As Nicolson wrote in *King George V*,

Scarcely however had the King arrived at Balmoral in the early morning of Saturday August 22nd when a telephone message was received from Downing Street stating that his presence in London might after all become necessary. The King at once decided that 'there was no use shilly-shallying on an occasion like this', and that he would return to London that very night. His Majesty reached Euston shortly after eight on the morning of Sunday August 23rd: two and half hours later he received the Prime Minister at Buckingham Palace.

Notes

1. MacDonald's private diary reveals that Harvey and Peacock 'could hold out for four days'.
2. *Hansard*, 8 September 1931.
3. Harold Nicolson, *King George V* (London, 1952).
4. Philip Snowden, *Autobiography* (London, 1934), p. 944.
5. Beatrice Webb, *The Diaries 1924-32* (ed. M.I. Cole) (London, 1956), p. 282.
6. Keith Feiling, *Life of Neville Chamberlain* (London, 1946).
7. Iain Macleod, *Neville Chamberlain* (London, 1961).
8. Cabinet minutes 22 August; R. Bassett, *1931: Political Crisis* (London, 1958), p. 122; Keith Middlemas and John Barnes, *Baldwin – A Biography* (London, 1969), p. 625; Philip Snowden, *Autobiography* (London, 1934), p. 945 *et alia*.
9. *Hansard*, 8 September 1931.
10. Ibid.
11. Robert Rhodes James, *Memoirs of a Conservative* (London, 1969), p. 367.

9 SUNDAY 23 AUGUST

MacDonald told the King that the government was urgently trying to negotiate for loans or credits of £80 million in New York and Paris. The government had been told that a precondition of the release of any such funds was a balanced budget, and they had asked the Bank of England to enquire whether economies of £76.5 million, including a 10 per cent cut in unemployment benefit, and further additional taxation of a similar amount, would create sufficient confidence for a loan to be forthcoming. An answer was expected before midnight. The Prime Minister told the King that he thought that many of his senior colleagues, including Henderson and Graham, would not agree to implement these cuts and that if they were to resign, the resignation of the Labour government as a whole would be inevitable. MacDonald therefore advised the King to see Baldwin and Sir Herbert Samuel. The King agreed, and according to MacDonald's diary,

> He said that he would advise them strongly to support me . . . He said that he believed I was the only person who could carry the country through. I said that did I share his belief I should not contemplate what I do, but that I did not share it.

Naturally it was the King's intention to see Baldwin first. He was not only Leader of the Opposition, he was also a former Prime Minister. However, shortly before Sir Clive Wigram, the King's Private Secretary, telephoned Davidson's house to ask Baldwin to go to the Palace, Baldwin had left to see Geoffrey Dawson, an old friend and the editor of *The Times*, at his house. Baldwin wanted to seek his advice and they stayed talking at Dawson's house until lunchtime, when they drove down to the Travellers Club. It was here that Baldwin was eventually tracked down and it was agreed that the King would see him at 3 p.m. Quite by chance, therefore, the King saw Sir Herbert Samuel first, at midday.

Although the sequence of interviews was fortuitous, it could hardly have had more important consequences. Baldwin, the previous evening, had been most dubious about the merits of a National government. After he had talked with Dawson they both agreed that it would be best if the Labour government were to reverse its policy of extravagance. Baldwin also discussed with Dawson the possibility of having to form his own administration. Shortly before he left to see the King, Baldwin wrote to his wife:

> I see the King at 3 o'clock . . . The crisis will now be a short one. We shall know tomorrow whether the P.M. will carry on to meet the House. If he can, I shall probably be able to come out in two or three days. If he throws his hand in I don't know what will happen.

He did not refer to the possibility of a National government.

By contrast, Samuel had told the King at noon that, in his view, the best solution would be for a Labour government, with the same members or reconstructed, to carry out the necessary economies. Failing that he favoured a National government composed of all three parties with MacDonald as Prime Minister. He did not favour a purely Conservative government, because he doubted its ability to attract enough popular support to get the necessary measures through.

Sir Clive Wigram records:

> Some time after the crisis, in discussing it with the King, I was impressed by the fact that his Majesty found Sir Herbert Samuel the clearest minded of the three and said that he had put the case for a National Government much clearer than either of the others. It was after the King's interview with Sir Herbert Samuel that His Majesty became convinced of the necessity for the National Government. It was quite by luck that Mr Baldwin did not come to see the King before Sir Herbert Samuel. I tried to catch the former, but found that he was out and so summoned Sir Herbert Samuel instead. Consequently by the time the King saw Mr Baldwin, His Majesty had had his talk with Sir Herbert Samuel.

The King had also, it will be recalled, according to MacDonald's diary, expressed the view that MacDonald was the only man who could see the country through when he had seen the Prime Minister at 10.30 a.m. Samuel, therefore, strongly reinforced what had been the King's first instinct.

It was no doubt for this reason that when Baldwin was received at Buckingham Palace at 3 p.m. he was first of all asked by the King whether he would be prepared to serve in a National government under Ramsay MacDonald. Baldwin replied that he would be ready to do anything to serve the country in the present crisis. If MacDonald insisted on resigning he would be prepared to form a government if he could be assured of the support of the Liberal Party. Once the economic crisis was over he would ask the King for a dissolution. To this the King agreed. 'The King', wrote Sir Clive Wigram, 'was greatly pleased with Mr Baldwin's readiness to meet the crisis which had arisen, and to sink Party interests for the sake of the Country.' (The full minutes of the Cabinet meetings held on 23 and 24 August 1931 are reproduced in Appendix II, p. 122 and Appendix IV, p. 130.

Everything now depended upon what happened at the Cabinet meeting at 7 p.m. According to the Greenwood Memorandum, proceedings began with a statement from the Prime Minister 'placing before Members the alternatives of the provisional scheme, including the 10% cut or a moratorium'. The same document continues: 'The discussion was interrupted to await the reply of New York on the suggestion.' Snowden in his autobiography indicated that so far the Bank of England had only received a personal reply by telephone from George L. Harrison, the President of the Federal Reserve Bank, who had said 'while he was not in a position to give the answer until he had consulted his financial associates, his opinion was that it would give satisfactory assurance and the credits would be forthcoming.' The message that was awaited was a personal cable from Harrison to the Prime Minister. (Harold Nicolson wrongly stated that the message waited for and eventually received was from J.P. Morgan.) The Cabinet reassembled at 9.10 p.m. since a telephone message had been received at No. 10 from the Bank of England saying that a cable had arrived from New York and that Sir Ernest Harvey was on his way to Downing Street with it. When Sir Ernest arrived, the Prime Minister left the Cabinet Room, took the cable from Harvey, re-entered the Cabinet

Room and read out the cable to the Ministers. The contents of the
cable, which was addressed to the Prime Minister by Harrison, may
be summarised as follows. No definite assurance could be given immediately on a joint French/American credit. If a public loan were needed
no favourable reaction could be predicted until Parliament were to
meet and pass the economy measures. A short-term Treasury operation
would be easier. They had discussed the possibility of raising 100
million to 150 million dollars in the form of 90-day Treasury Bills
subject to renewals for an inclusive period of one year. It was assumed
as a condition that the French banking market would do the same. The
cable ended with the words:

Are we right in assuming that the programme under consideration
will have the sincere approval and support of the Bank of England
and the City generally and thus go a long way towards restoring
internal confidence in Great Britain? Of course our ability to do
anything depends on the response of public opinion, particularly
in Great Britain to the Government's announcement of the programme.

The message from Harrison is appended in full to the Cabinet minutes
of 23 August, and appears in Appendix III on p. 128.

Nicolson wrote: 'he [the Prime Minister] read the telegram slowly
to his assembled colleagues, and when he reached the concluding sentence loud protests were raised. To Sir Ernest Harvey, waiting in the
adjoining room it seemed that "pandemonium had broken out".' After
the communication had been read, according to Nicolson, the Prime
Minister made a strong appeal to his colleagues to accept the proposals
about which the enquiry had been made. Although he was only too
well aware that there would be much resentment in Labour circles he
was sure that the majority of the party would accept the proposals if
he were able to put the full facts before them. Moral prestige would be
lost if the unemployed were left in a privileged position. Therefore he
asked the Cabinet there and then to agree to a 10 per cent cut in
unemployment relief, and if any senior Minister felt it necessary to
resign rather than consent to such a measure, then the whole government must resign. Although there have been conflicting reports, it is

generally accepted that nine Ministers voted against these proposals. They were Henderson, Lansbury, Clynes, Graham, Alexander, Greenwood, Johnston, Adamson and Addison. Eleven Ministers, including the Prime Minister, voted in favour of accepting the 10 per cent unemployment cut: they were Sankey, Snowden, Passfield (Sidney Webb), Thomas, Shaw, Wedgwood Benn, Amulree, Lees-Smith, Miss Bondfield and Herbert Morrison. The Cabinet minute simply states:

> Each member of the Cabinet then expressed his view on the question of the inclusion or otherwise in the proposals of the 10% reduction in Unemployment. Indications were given that a majority of the Cabinet favoured the inclusion in the economy proposals of the 10% cut but that this would involve the resignation of certain Ministers from the Government.

MacDonald reported to the King that the voting was eleven for acceptance and eight against, but that still leaves one vote unaccounted for and Lord Parmoor was the only absentee. The Greenwood Memorandum without mentioning either names or numbers states:

> A minority of the Cabinet opposed the 10% cut. The majority held that the Government could only adopt this proposal if there was complete or almost complete unanimity in the Cabinet. Everybody agreed that the position was such that it was impossible to continue.

Snowden wrote in his autobiography:

> When this final disagreement occurred it was evident that the Prime Minister had anticipated such a development and had made his plans to deal with it. He asked the members of the Cabinet to place their resignations in his hands. This was done and the Prime Minister immediately left the meeting to seek an audience with the King to acquaint him with the position and to advise His Majesty to hold a conference with Mr Baldwin, Sir Herbert Samuel and himself next morning. The Cabinet agreed to this course. Mr MacDonald left at 10.10 p.m. and the members of the Cabinet remained in the room to await his return. He came back at 10.40 and told us that His Majesty

had accepted his advice to meet Mr Baldwin, Sir Herbert Samuel and himself next morning at 10 o'clock.

Snowden's account of what happened at this crucial Cabinet meeting omits the very strong plea from MacDonald for Cabinet unity which was recorded both in the Cabinet minutes and by Harold Nicolson. We must now see what had happened at the Palace. At 10.10 MacDonald had left the Cabinet Room. Sir Ernest Harvey was still at 10 Downing Street at the time. He describes the Prime Minister as being in a state of extreme agitation, shouting as he passed: 'I am off to the Palace to throw in my hand.' The Prime Minister reached the Palace at 10.20 p.m.

Sir Clive Wigram, the King's Private Secretary, wrote:

The Prime Minister looked scared and unbalanced. He told the King that all was up and that at the Cabinet 11 had voted for accepting the terms of the Bankers and 8 against. The opposition included Henderson, Graham, Adamson, Greenwood, Clynes, Alexander, Addison and Lansbury. In these circumstances the Prime Minister had no alternative than to tender the resignation of the Cabinet.

The King impressed on the Prime Minister that he was the only man to lead the country through this crisis and hoped that he would reconsider the situation. His Majesty told him that the Conservatives and Liberals would support him in restoring the confidence of foreigners in the country.

The Prime Minister asked whether the King would confer with Baldwin, Samuel and himself in the morning. His Majesty willingly acceded to this request. The Prime Minister telephoned to Downing Street to ask his Private Secretary to arrange for Baldwin and Samuel to meet him as soon as possible.

Harold Nicolson wrongly states in *King George V* that by then the Cabinet had dispersed and that even Snowden had gone to bed. This is an extraordinary error of fact. As we have already seen, Snowden described MacDonald's return to the Cabinet, which did not adjourn for another ten minutes, in his autobiography which was published nearly twenty years before Nicolson's life of King George. Not only did

MacDonald return to his colleagues but he arranged for a further Cabinet meeting to be held at 12 noon the following day, 24 August. It is important for Nicolson to be corrected since his version of events would lead, and probably has led, many people to assume that MacDonald did not inform his colleagues that the King had agreed to see himself, Baldwin and Samuel the following morning, a request which they had supported him in making, whereas, in fact, on Snowden's evidence, he had. The Cabinet minutes confirm that Snowden's account was substantially correct but also recorded a decision 'that the Prime Minister should inform the Opposition Party leaders of the nature of the message he had received from Mr Harrison' (see Appendix II, p. 122).

At 10.44 p.m., about five minutes before the Cabinet dispersed, Sir Herbert Samuel arrived at 10 Downing Street. At 11.10 Baldwin arrived and was followed a few minutes later by Neville Chamberlain. Sir Joseph Stamp and two Directors of the Bank of England arrived, but only stayed for about a quarter of an hour. The Opposition leaders left at about 12.15 a.m. and no statement was issued on their departure. As to what took place at this meeting, we must rely on the diaries of Neville Chamberlain and the draft memoirs of Lord Davidson. After MacDonald had told the gathering of the earlier Cabinet meeting and of the agreement of the King to see the three party leaders the following morning, Chamberlain wrote:

For himself, he would help us to get these proposals through, though it means his death warrant, but it would be of no use for him to join a Government. He would be a ridiculous figure unable to command support and would bring odium on us as well as himself . . . I then intervened . . . had he considered that though not commanding many votes in the House he might command much support in the country. And would not a Government including members of all Parties hold a much stronger position than a two-party combination. R.M. said that his mind was not finally made up but that was his present mood. I then suggested that many people would not understand why, if he supported the new Government, he refused to enter it and would be criticised on that ground. He replied that that was a worrying point but people would say he had stuck to office for the sake of the salary, to which I replied that if several of his colleagues accompanied him the odium would, at least, be spread. Finally I asked him if he had considered the effect on foreign opinion which was all important . . . This argument took him in a weak place. He said, without egotism he thought his name did carry weight in America. Samuel supported me strongly though S.B. maintained silence and we did not pursue the matter further then.

Davidson wrote in his draft memoirs:

Shortly after the Cabinet dispersed S.B. went to Downing Street in response to a request from MacDonald, Samuel had already arrived and within a few minutes they were joined by Neville Chamberlain and Josiah Stamp. MacDonald told them of the situation in the Cabinet, and of his advice to the King. It was quite clear that he intended to resign and that he had no intention of joining in a Coalition, even though the King had urged him to head one. Neville, however, pressed on him the support in the country that he would bring to such an administration and the effect it would have in restoring confidence. His arguments seemed to have no effect. To everyone else at the meeting it seemed quite certain that MacDonald intended to resign, and S.B. returned from it convinced that he would have to form a Government. Nor did he think it a bad thing since, as I had emphasized before, he had little love for Coalitions.

Since Baldwin was staying at Davidson's house this record is likely to be accurate. Malcolm MacDonald has informed the author that late at night on 23 August (it was probably in the early hours of 24 August since the party leaders did not leave Downing Street until 12.15) his father spoke to him on the telephone at Lossiemouth and told him that he would be resigning as Prime Minister and would return to Lossiemouth the following day. MacDonald's own uncertainty of mind is contained in his private diary for 23 August. He described the Cabinet vote and his audience with the King and noted that he would be meeting the party leaders and the King on the following day. However he also wrote,

Am preparing a statement if I resign to give to the Press at once. I commit political suicide to save the crisis. If there is no other way I shall do it as cheerfully as an ancient Jap. The Mistress of Upp Frog Lodge has returned and is making love to me. How few people understand the unattractiveness of this place and this office to me.

Upper Frognal Lodge was his private home in Hampstead and by 'this place' he presumably meant 10 Downing Street. It is not clear what he meant by 'political suicide'. The most reasonable assumption is to conclude that he was referring to the National Government and his decision to lead it, which was made the following day, but this robs his following sentence of any meaning. He was plainly on the verge of complete nervous exhaustion.

From this account it is clear beyond reasonable doubt that there was no prearranged plan involving MacDonald and the other party leaders for the formation of a National government. This is not, of course, to say that nobody wished to see a National government and a government headed by MacDonald. It is clear that Neville Chamberlain wanted this very strongly and did all that he could to persuade MacDonald to accept this proposal, but, as Chamberlain confessed in a speech at Dumfries on 12 September, he thought, when he left 10 Downing Street at 12.15 a.m. on 24 August, that his attempts at persuasion had failed. Sir Herbert Samuel, too, strongly favoured a National government with MacDonald as Prime Minister and through a fortuity, which nobody could have foreseen, strengthened the King in his belief that this would be desirable when he went to the Palace before Baldwin. It is quite clear that Baldwin did not favour a National government. He was alone among the political leaders in making no attempt to persuade MacDonald to remain Prime Minister. Even when directly asked by the King if he would agree to serve in a National government under MacDonald, he had replied somewhat indirectly that he would be ready to do anything to serve the country in the present crisis. He went on to say that he would, if granted a dissolution when the crisis was over, be prepared to form an administration himself if he could be assured of the support of the Liberal Party.

As for Ramsay MacDonald, it would be absurd to pretend that the possibility of a National government had never crossed his mind. In an *unprecedented* situation such as existed, no possibility could be excluded, except of course that the Labour government could continue. Despite earlier allegations, often based on mere gossip and innuendo, MacDonald is first recorded as mentioning the possibility at a meeting on 21 August with Chamberlain, Samuel and Sir Samuel Hoare when, in what Chamberlain's diary calls a jocular way, he said: 'Well, are you prepared to join the Board of Directors?' This was between 5 p.m. and 7 p.m. on Friday 21 August, but at a later meeting with Chamberlain and Hoare on that same evening, in Hoare's words, 'the conclusion that Chamberlain and I drew from them [his words] was the same. He had decided to resign and to advise the King to send for the party leaders for consultations as to the next step.' On the evening of Saturday 22 August, Ramsay MacDonald spoke to his son Malcolm, saying that he would cease to be Prime Minister, would sit on the Opposition benches of the House of Commons but supporting the economic cuts which he had favoured in the Labour Cabinet. Finally, in the early hours of 24 August Baldwin, Chamberlain, Samuel and MacDonald's son Malcolm were all convinced that he would resign later that day.

On the morning of 24 August, according to Malcolm MacDonald, Ramsay MacDonald telephoned to his daughter Ishbel. He told her that the King had implored him to form a National government. Malcolm MacDonald noted,

> Yet J.R.M. knows what the Country needs and wants in this crisis, and it is a question whether it is not his duty to form a Government representative of all three parties to tide over a few weeks, till the danger of a financial crash is past — and damn the consequences to himself after that.

MacDonald's mind had evidently clarified somewhat since the previous night.

10 MONDAY 24 AUGUST

At 10 a.m. on Monday 24 August the King saw the Prime Minister and the other two leaders. His diary states:

At 10.0 I held a Conference here in the Indian Room with Prime Minister, Baldwin and Samuel and we discussed the formation of a National Government composed of all three Parties with Ramsay MacDonald as PM, as a temporary measure to pass the necessary Economy and Finance Bill through the House of Commons when there would be a dissolution followed by a General Election and this we agreed to . . . The Prime Minister came at 4.0 and tendered his resignation. I then invited him to form a National Government which he agreed to do.

Sir Clive Wigram wrote the following detailed memorandum:

At 10 am the King held a Conference at Buckingham Palace at which the Prime Minister, Baldwin and Samuel were present. At the beginning His Majesty impressed upon them that before they left the Palace some communique must be issued, which would no longer keep the country and the world in suspense. The Prime Minister said that he had the resignation of his Cabinet in his pocket, but the King replied that he trusted that there was no question of the Prime Minister's resignation: the leaders of the three Parties must get together and come to some arrangement. His Majesty hoped that the Prime Minister with the colleagues who remained faithful to him, would help in the formation of a National Government, which the King was sure would be supported by the Conservatives and the Liberals. The King assured the Prime Minister that, remaining at his post, his position and reputation would be much more enhanced than if he surrendered the government of the Country at such a crisis. Baldwin and Samuel said that they were willing to serve under the Prime Minister, and render all help possible to carry on the

Government as a National Emergency Government until a bill or bills had been passed by Parliament which would restore once more British credit and the confidence of foreigners. After that they would expect His Majesty to grant a dissolution. To this course the King agreed. During the Election the National Government would remain in being, though, of course, each Party would fight the Election on its own lines.

At 10.35 am the King left the three Party leaders to settle the details of the communique to be issued, and the latter said that they would let His Majesty know when they were ready.

About 11.45 the King was requested to return to the Conference and was glad to hear that they had been able to some extent to come to some arrangement. A Memorandum had been drawn up which Baldwin and Samuel could place before their respective Parties but the Prime Minister said that he would not read this out in Cabinet as he should keep it only for those who remained faithful to him. Probably the New National Government would consist of a small Cabinet of 12. It is quite understood that, up to now, the Cabinet had not resigned. His Majesty congratulated them on the solution of this difficult problem and pointed out that while France and other countries existed for weeks without a Government, in this country our constitution is so generous that leaders of Parties, after fighting one another for months in the House of Commons, were ready to meet together under the roof of the Sovereign and sink their own differences for a common good and arrange to meet one of the gravest crises that the British Empire had yet been asked to face.

At the end of the conference the following communiqué was issued to the Press: 'His Majesty the King invited the Prime Minister, Mr Stanley Baldwin and Sir Herbert Samuel to Buckingham Palace this morning, and the formation of a National Government is under consideration. A fuller announcement will be made later.' The agreed memorandum referred to by Sir Clive Wigram reads as follows:

(1)   National Government to be formed to deal with the present financial emergency

(2)   It will not be a Coalition in the ordinary sense of the term, but

cooperation of individuals

(3)   When the emergency is dealt with, the Government's work will have finished and the Parties will return to their ordinary position

(4)   The economies and imports shall be equitable and shall generally follow the lines of the suggestions attached, designed to enable a loan to be raised in New York and Paris

(5)   If there is any legislation which is necessary to pass for special departmental or other reasons and it is generally accepted by the different Parties it may be undertaken

(6)   The Cabinet shall be reduced to a minimum.

The Cabinet met at twelve noon. A great many totally inaccurate accounts of what occurred were given by some of those present. It is therefore necessary to state what was recorded in the official Cabinet minutes (which appear in full in Appendix IV, p. 130). The Prime Minister informed the Cabinet that he had met the King, Stanley Baldwin and Sir Herbert Samuel at 10 o'clock that morning. He is quoted in the minutes as saying: 'The proposal was that His Majesty should invite certain individuals to take upon their shoulders the burden of carrying on the Government and Mr Baldwin and Sir Herbert Samuel had stated that they were prepared to act accordingly.' The Prime Minister 'then stated that he proposed to tender to His Majesty the resignation of the Government'. MacDonald then went on to say:

He had not failed to present the case against his participation in the proposed Administration but, in view of the gravity of the situation he had felt that there was no other course open to him than to assist in the formation of a National Government on a comprehensive basis for the purpose of meeting the emergency.

MacDonald did not specifically state that he was to be the Prime Minister in the new National administration, although this was assumed, and it will be noted that he in fact did read out the memorandum which Samuel had drafted and which Baldwin and Samuel had presented to their followers, despite the fact that he told the King that he would not do so. There would be a small Cabinet of 12, which would not exist for a period longer than was necessary to dispose of the emergency and when that purpose was achieved, the political parties would resume their respective positions. The administration would not be a coalition government, but a government of co-operation for this one purpose. A general election would follow at the end of the emergency period and there would be no coupons, pacts or other party arrangements. The Prime Minister added that he would try to avoid by-election contests in the emergency but if they had to take place the leaders could send messages to their party candidates. He singled out Herbert Morrison's Transport Bill as a measure which would be passed. The members of the Cabinet expressed a wish that their resignations should be tendered as soon as possible and it was agreed that the Prime Minister should do so that afternoon and that arrangements should be made for them to surrender their seals of office at the earliest opportunity. It was agreed that all resigning Ministers could retain their copies of the Cabinet Papers for the period during which they had sat in the Cabinet, as is the usual custom. It was however pointed out that the original paper containing economies which the Cabinet Economic Committee had put forward had, for security reasons, been returned to the Deputy Secretary to the Cabinet immediately after the Cabinet meeting held on 19 August. It was agreed that this document would be re-issued to each member of the existing Cabinet. Finally the Lord Chancellor moved and the Cabinet accepted that it 'placed on record their warm appreciation of the great kindness, consideration and courtesy invariably shown by the Prime Minister, when presiding over their meetings and conducting the business of the Cabinet'. It must be doubted whether such a motion could have been moved and carried at the end of an acrimonious meeting.

In dealing with the 1931 crisis, Harold Nicolson in his book *King George V* acknowledged that he had had verbal discussions with certain named people – Lord Wigram, Lord Hardinge of Penshurst, Lord Samuel, Sir Ernest Harvey, Sir Edward Peacock and Herbert Morrison. The latter was the only member of the Labour Cabinet. Nicolson wrote:

> Mr Ramsay MacDonald left Buckingham Palace at 11.55 and his last meeting with his colleagues took place at noon. He entered the Cabinet room with a confident, or as one of his colleagues described it, a

'jaunty' air, and at once informed the assembled Ministers that it had been decided to form a 'Cabinet of Individuals' to deal with the emergency. He himself was to be one of these 'individuals'; he invited anyone who so desired to join him in this patriotic act of self sacrifice. There was a hush when he made this astounding announcement. Mr Arthur Henderson flung himself back in his chair and emitted a low whistle. Mr Herbert Morrison, at that date a very junior Minister, broke the silence with the words 'Well, Prime Minister, it is very easy to get in to such a combination: you will find it very difficult to get out of it. And I for one am not coming with you.' One by one around the table each of the Ministers signified his unwillingness to join. Mr Ramsay MacDonald found himself almost deserted except by Mr Thomas, Lord Sankey and an almost unwilling Philip Snowden. The Cabinet dispersed at 12.25.[1]

Nicolson states in a footnote[2] that he only departed from his practice of recording such facts or opinions as can be confirmed by documentary evidence in describing the events leading up to the formation of the National government and named his verbal informants. From the list it is clear that his informant on the Cabinet meeting must have been Herbert Morrison since none of the other named people could have been present. It is highly significant that in Nicolson's account the only remark attributed to any individual member of the Cabinet was allegedly made by Morrison and that it took the form of a violent denunciation of the proposed National government. Morrison's highly ambivalent attitude towards the National government is fully described in the book *Herbert Morrison* by Donoughue and Jones; the authors make it clear that Morrison very nearly joined the National government and they wrote:

One is led to suspect that he [Morrison] was not telling the truth about his first reaction. Indeed F. George Kay who 'ghosted' Morrison's Autobiography claims that Morrison told him that he had at first wanted to join MacDonald and had asked to be taken in.[3]

Mr Alistair MacDonald has recalled overhearing a telephone conversation between his father and Herbert Morrison in which Ramsay

MacDonald strongly advised Morrison not to join the National government.

The Cabinet minutes do not record Morrison or any individual
Minister as making any comment on MacDonald's statement. Strong
statements of dissent are normally recorded in Cabinet minutes. There
is no record in the Cabinet minutes of MacDonald inviting any of his
colleagues to join the National government. When each member of a
Cabinet is asked to state his views on a subject the matter is invariably
recorded in Cabinet minutes, although it is not the practice to record
a formal vote. There is no such record in the Cabinet minutes for 24
August. Nicolson wrote his life of King George V in 1952, when
Morrison was Deputy Leader of the Labour Party and was hoping to
succeed Attlee as the Leader. One can only conclude that Morrison
deliberately gave Nicolson a false account of what occurred at this
Cabinet meeting in 1931 in order to advance his own prospects of
becoming Leader of the Labour Party after Attlee retired in 1955. By
the time that his own autobiography was 'ghosted' Morrison had
retired from active politics. In fact MacDonald did not at the Cabinet
meeting request any of his colleagues to join him in the National
government. After the meeting he asked Snowden, Thomas and Sankey
to join him and they agreed to do so.

Philip Snowden was guilty of a more pardonable error. In his autobiography[4] he stated that he was only prepared to join the National
government, and so informed the Prime Minister, when he was invited
to remain Chancellor after the Cabinet was over, subject to his being
satisfied as to the following conditions:

(1)   That the new Administration would not exist for a longer
      period than to dispose of the emergency, and that when that
      was achieved the political parties would assume their respec-
      tive positions

(2)   That the Administration would not be a Coalition Government
      in the general sense of the term but a National Government for
      one purpose only

(3)   That as soon as the financial crisis had been settled there
      should be a General Election and at that Election there would
      be no merging of political parties and no 'coupon' or other

party arrangement

(4) That the Administration which was being formed would not propose any party legislation of a controversial character but would continue itself to the one purpose for which it was being formed.

Snowden was however merely quoting word for word the minuted statement of the Prime Minister at the final Cabinet meeting of the Labour government. By the time Snowden wrote his autobiography he had resigned from the National government and MacDonald was being branded as a traitor to his party. Snowden was thus establishing the purity of his own motives by quoting verbatim and in public, as his precondition for joining the National government, conditions which the Prime Minister had already privately revealed to the Labour Cabinet but was precluded from making public in order to expose Snowden since it would have been a serious breach of Cabinet confidentiality, reprehensible in an ex-Minister as Snowden then was, but unpardonable in a ruling Prime Minister. At 4.10 p.m. on 24 August 1931 Ramsay MacDonald tendered the resignation of the Labour government and kissed hands in accepting the King's Commission to become Prime Minister of a new National government.

Notes

1. Harold Nicolson, *King George V* (London, 1952), p. 467.
2. Nicolson, *King George V*, p. 462.
3. B. Donoughue and G.M. Jones, *Herbert Morrison* (London, 1973), chapter on 'The 1931 Crisis'.
4. Philip Snowden, *Autobiography* (London, 1934), p. 955.

11 THE RECRIMINATIONS

Immediately after the National government was formed recriminations began. Ironically the bitterest critic proved to be Snowden, who joined MacDonald in the National government and parted company from him a year later.

Snowden, on the basis of the most slender evidence, sought to prove in his autobiography[1] that.

> Taking all these things together, I think they give ground for the suspicion expressed by Mr Henderson and other Labour Ministers that Mr MacDonald had deliberately planned the scheme of a National Government, which would at the same time enable him to retain the position of Prime Minister and to associate with political colleagues with whom he was more in sympathy than he had ever been with his Labour colleagues . . . His mind for a long time before this crisis arose had been turning to the idea of a new Party orientation and government by what he called a Council of State. Something of this sort had not altogether been absent from the mind of Mr Baldwin, for I remember a statement he made two or three years before, that probably the time was not far distant when he and Mr MacDonald would be sitting in the same Cabinet. This observation was probably due to Mr Baldwin's shrewd appreciation of Mr MacDonald's political temperament.

This is a most astonishing paragraph. What are 'all these things' which when taken together lead to so positive a conclusion? First, Snowden appears to have been surprised that the Prime Minister had anticipated the final disagreement and had made his plans to deal with it, which were to ask the members of the Cabinet for their resignations and to advise the King to hold a conference with Mr Baldwin, Sir Herbert Samuel and himself on the following morning. However, what Mr Snowden knew, and his readers did not, was that a Cabinet minute for the meeting held on the morning of Saturday 22 August read as follows:

The Prime Minister asked the Cabinet to authorise him to put to the Opposition leaders an extra £20 million made up of £12½ million, the 10% cut in Benefit and £7¾ million in other ways. The Cabinet were not prepared to authorise the Prime Minister to make this offer. The Chancellor of the Exchequer and the Secretary of State for Dominion Affairs [J.H. Thomas] asked that their dissent from this conclusion be recorded.

Cabinet minutes are circulated the following day and, in any event, the Labour Cabinet finally met before voting on the issue of unemployment benefit at 7 p.m. on Sunday 23 August. Could any reasonable man have supposed that there was the smallest chance of the Labour government surviving after that Cabinet decision had been taken? MacDonald told the King on the following morning that he thought that many of his colleagues would resign if these cuts in unemployment benefit were made and that this would make inevitable the resignation of the Labour government. The King had suggested to the Prime Minister that he should see the other party leaders and a statement had been issued from Buckingham Palace on the morning of Sunday 23 August in the following terms: 'On the Prime Minister's advice the King has asked Mr Baldwin and Sir Herbert Samuel to see him, because His Majesty wishes to hear from them themselves what the position of their respective Parties is.'

There was no criticism voiced when the Cabinet met at 7 p.m. on 23 August at the advice given by MacDonald to the King. The development anticipated by the Prime Minister and the plans that he had made to deal with it would have been taken by any person who was not of subnormal intelligence. What evidence did Snowden have that MacDonald's mind had been turning to the idea of a new party orientation by what he called a Council of State? MacDonald had only once used the term 'Council of State'. This was in his reply to the debate on the King's Speech in June 1929 when he had, for the second time, become Prime Minister of a minority Labour government. He then said,

I wonder how far it is possible, without abandoning any of our party positions . . . to consider ourselves more of a Council of State and less as arrayed regiments facing each other in battle . . . so that by putting our ideas into a common pool we can bring out from that common pool legislation and administration that will be of substantial benefit for the nation as a whole?

Any reader of this speech will quickly see that the new Prime Minister was frankly recognising the problems posed for all minority governments. For this speech to be dredged up several years later with the implication that MacDonald favoured the replacement of normal parliamentary government by a newly created institution called a Council of State is indicative of the poverty of the case that Snowden was attempting to put forward.

It would be interesting to know when Baldwin made the alleged statement about himself and MacDonald sitting in the same Cabinet, and to whom. It seems most unlikely that Baldwin ever spoke in this vein to Davidson, his closest confidant, or to Neville Chamberlain, his principal lieutenant. Indeed, he did not disguise from either his dislike of coalitions, to the intense irritation of Neville Chamberlain on the evening of Saturday 22 August. It would be interesting to know with whom Snowden believed MacDonald had been deliberately planning 'the scheme of a National Government'. Certainly Neville Chamberlain made every attempt to persuade MacDonald to support the concept, but until the very end Chamberlain believed that he had been rebuffed. From Snowden's two-volume autobiography, one may conclude that his long-standing personal dislike of MacDonald, together with his bitterness at the decision of the National government to introduce a revenue tariff against which he had fought so implacably, and a desire to rehabilitate his reputation with his former colleagues, led him on the most slender evidence, if indeed it can be so termed, to charge MacDonald with what others had already said and what he now wished to believe.

Sidney and Beatrice Webb's charges against MacDonald also require some examination. In the *Political Quarterly* early in 1932 Sidney Webb wrote of 'the whole unfolding within sixty-three days of a single drama, in all its development foreseen in advance, it is safe to say, only by the statesman who was at once its author, its producer, and its principal actor'. He suggested that the idea of a National government seemed 'to have been germinating in the Prime Minister's mind for months before the blow was struck'. Both the Webbs subsequently attached a sinister interpretation to a letter written by MacDonald to Sidney Webb on 14 July 1931, apparently to wish him a happy birthday, since it starts with 'I am so sorry that I did not know that yesterday was your birthday.' Later on in the letter MacDonald writes, 'As you know, I am having the most awful difficulty about the House of Lords . . . The solution will have to come. I am afraid by moves which will surprise all of you. I am still working on it however.' This was an obvious reference to the weakness of Labour's representation in the House of Lords. An interpretation given to it at the time by the Webbs was that MacDonald himself might go to the House of Lords, possibly as Foreign Secretary. This was certainly a plausible, but not very likely, possibility.

In her diary of 27 August 1931 Beatrice Webb wrote:

Arnold reports that Lansbury told him that JRM spoke to him casually at the end of July as a result of the issue of the May report, as to the desirability of a National Government if the financial position became serious. Lansbury rejected the notion as impossible and JRM dropped the question. By the light of this incident the PM's letter to SW July 14, which puzzled us, seems to indicate some such solution, put forward tentatively. 'You may think that I have been doing nothing', he wrote, 'but as a matter of fact I have been working at it for weekend after weekend and I am at a complete dead end. We have not the material in our party that we ought to have. The solution will have to come, I am afraid, by moves which will surprise you. I am still working on it however.'

This paragraph contains two features which those who are familiar with the diaries of Beatrice Webb will recognise. All too often she is ready to quote remarks made by a third party to a second without troubling to check with the author of the remark as to whether it was accurate or not. It would have been perfectly easy to have asked Lansbury whether or not MacDonald spoke to him in the terms which Arnold alleged. She is also not immune from the selective quotation. In her diary entry of 27 August 1931 she omitted the vital sentence in MacDonald's letter to her husband: 'As you know, I am having the most awful difficulty about the House of Lords.' If this is related to her quotation from the 14 July letter in her diary of 27 August it is quite clear that when MacDonald wrote, 'we have not the material in our Party that we ought to have' he was in fact referring to the House of Lords, and therefore when put in its true context the quotation has no bearing on the formation of the National government at all. Sidney Webb's memory has been shown to be unreliable. The diaries of Beatrice Webb are in many ways fascinating to read, if only because of the passages of unconscious self-revelation, but they are too careless and unreliable as to what may or may not have happened on a particular day to be an acceptable source of fact unless corroborated by identical evidence from a totally independent origin. Forty-seven years later, a perfectly innocent explanation can be provided for MacDonald's letter of 14 July which so puzzled Sidney and Beatrice Webb, and which she sought to use as evidence that MacDonald was already planning the formation of the National government. There is an entry in MacDonald's private diary for 14 July 1931 which reads: 'Last night Henderson came to discuss Geneva and amongst other things proposed that I should be a delegate to the Disarmament Conference. I also mentioned his going to the Lords.' It is clear that MacDonald was in fact trying to strengthen the House of Lords by promoting Henderson to the Upper House.

There is one other inaccurate source which must be named and then discarded. From 1924 to 1931 Macneill Weir was Parliamentary Private Secretary to Ramsay MacDonald. Shortly after the death of MacDonald, Weir published a book called *The Tragedy of Ramsay MacDonald*.[2] As its title indicates, this book is not flattering to MacDonald. The author has read it with great care and in particular has studied the chapters dealing with the events which occurred between 31 July and 24 August 1931 more than once. He has compared the allegations made by Weir with the evidence, both verbal and written, from over forty different sources which have been available to him. Briefly, Weir maintained that Ramsay MacDonald left London for Lossiemouth when the House of Commons rose on 31 July knowing (indeed having planned) that his holiday would shortly be interrupted. Contingency plans had, it is true, been made for the emergency recall of parliamentary recess from July until the end of October. Yet according to Weir, 'MacDonald endeavoured to make it appear that the re-assembly of Parliament was uncertain, whereas he knew that it was definite and inevitable if his premeditated purpose had to be achieved.' He accuses MacDonald of entering into a conspiracy in advance with Snowden to destroy the Labour government and to replace it by a largely Conservative National government. He refers to a two-hour meeting between the two men during which MacDonald is supposed to have attempted to suborn Snowden. Such a meeting is not mentioned in Snowden's memoirs or in any other source of which the author is aware. Weir charges Sir Herbert Samuel with venality. He writes:

> When all hope of ever again enjoying the sweets of office had faded on the far horizon, suddenly, unexpectedly, Sir Herbert Samuel is asked to join in the negotiation which, at the worst, meant recognition and, at the best, might lead to high office. It is not surprising, having regard to the circumstances, personal and political, that Sir Herbert Samuel accepted with alacrity MacDonald's invitation to join the cabal.

If Weir genuinely believed that Sir Herbert Samuel was solely motivated by a desire for political office he might have addressed himself to the question of why Samuel declined Cabinet office at the hands of Lloyd George in 1916 and why, on the issue of protection, Samuel should having resigned as Home Secretary from the National government only twelve months after he had joined it. Weir later in his book refers to his return to 10 Downing Street on 24 August, since he was still Parliamentary Private Secretary to MacDonald. The new National Cabinet had met, so he said, for the first time. He states that Sir John Simon was there, and actually describes his emotions at seeing Simon at No. 10, but Sir John Simon was not a member of the first National government. He became Foreign Secretary in October 1931 after the general election. Nobody could, in any event, have been at 10 Downing Street attending a Cabinet meeting on 24 August 1931, since the first Cabinet meeting of the National government took place on 26 August.

It would not normally have been necessary to have dwelt for so long on one bitter and inaccurate book. However, the post of Parliamentary Private Secretary to the Prime Minister can be a political post of considerable influence. Such a person would normally be the recipient of highly confidential information. No student of these events could be blamed if he were to take for granted that any written statements made by Macneill Weir would be authentic and any views expressed would be authoritative. The mixture of fallacious speculation, malicious tendentiousness and carelessness in regard to fact has led the author to regard any evidence put forward by Macneill Weir as worthless.

The author has examined every other allegation, rumour, innuendo and piece of hearsay which is contained or alluded to in the bibliography attached to this book and they have reinforced the conclusion which he has reached. This conclusion can be simply stated. MacDonald had little or no knowledge of economic affairs; in these matters he was very much in the hands of Philip Snowden, the Chancellor of the Exchequer, the Bank of England and the Treasury.

The conduct of Ramsay MacDonald was in the author's view wholly honourable. It is necessary to state this, since he believes that the step which MacDonald took was profoundly mistaken. On Thursday 10 September, Philip Snowden, by then Chancellor of the Exchequer in the National government, presented what he described in his autobiography as 'the most momentous Budget ever submitted to the House of Commons in peacetime'. The much talked about deficit of £170 million was officially revealed for the first time to Parliament. Economy proposals of £70 million were approved and the sum set aside for Debt Remission was reduced from £50 million to £32 million. The sum to be raised in extra taxation amounted to £79 million. The conditions of the foreign bankers, the Bank of England, the Conservative and Liberal parties were fully met. Yet the withdrawal of funds from London, although greatly reduced since the formation of the National government, had never wholly stopped. On 16 September, only six days after the legislative measures for which George L. Harrison had asked were passed by Parliament, the withdrawals accelerated sharply. On 16 September, £5 million was withdrawn; on 17 September the figure had reached £10 million, on the 18th it was nearly £18 million and on Saturday 19 September, a half day, over £10 million was lost. The credits of £80 million for the sake of which the trauma had been enacted were nearly exhausted. On 19 September, the Bank of England advised the Prime Minister and the Chancellor to abandon the gold standard. An official statement was issued from 10 Downing Street on Sunday night, 20 September, saying that a Bill would be introduced and passed by Parliament through all its stages the following day. The main reason for the formation of the National government had evaporated but the inter-party bitterness was such that there could be no going back.

The person whose views have been most clearly vindicated was Ernest Bevin, who was largely responsible for the challenge mounted by the TUC General Council against the entire economic strategy of the government, the Bank of England, the Opposition parties and the foreign bankers. Some may find it ignominious to recall that the price to be paid for Britain remaining on the gold standard for an extra three and a half weeks involved the reduction of the rate of unemployment benefit for a man from 17 shillings weekly to 15*s*. 3*d*. (the final 10 per cent that brought down the Labour government). There was not much equality of sacrifice which reduced unemployment pay from such a pitifully low peak to a starvation existence, as compared with the reduction of the salary of a Cabinet Minister from £5,000 to £4,000. None of the ex-Ministers emerged with credit, particularly since they attempted to repudiate what they had already agreed in much the same way as some members of the former Labour Cabinet in 1971 approached the issue of the Common Market. It is an astonishing reflection on the level of the economic thinking of the Labour Cabinet that there were no resignations when Sir Oswald Mosley's proposals for creating 750,000 new jobs were rejected in 1930, and yet the entire Labour Cabinet resigned over a 10 per cent cut in unemployment pay one year later. The issue in 1931 was not between socialism and capitalism as mouthed on political platforms; it was rather between economic radicals and economic conservatives. In the event all three political parties proved to be the latter. Mosley was the chief economic radical in Parliament and he had already burned his boats. Bevin saw the issue with equal clarity and the irony was that when the Labour Party had for the first time in 1945 an overwhelming parliamentary majority, he was sent to the Foreign Office and not to the Treasury, where he rightly belonged.

Notes

1. Philip Snowden, *Autobiography* (London, 1934), p. 954.
2. L. Macneill Weir, *The Tragedy of Ramsay MacDonald* (London, 1938).

POSTSCRIPT

By the afternoon of Monday 24 August MacDonald was physically, emotionally and mentally exhausted. Since 17 August events had moved with such speed that he was not, at all times, capable of coherent thought. After the lapse of nearly fifty years, we can, perhaps, see more clearly than MacDonald was able to at the time how, and why, everything happened as it did.

First, it cannot be disputed that MacDonald, until the evening of 23 August, which was less than twenty-four hours before the National government was formed, repeatedly tried to keep his Cabinet united, and never more so than in his final attempt on the evening of 23 August. There is no doubt that MacDonald believed that the cuts of £76 million were essential to maintain the parity of the pound and that if the parity of the pound were not maintained, Britain would face ruin. This view was not contested by a single member of the Labour Cabinet at the time. Nobody in the Cabinet disputed that the parity of the pound must be held, although, as we have seen, the TUC, under the strong influence of Ernest Bevin, did not believe that it would be a disaster if Britain were forced off the gold standard. The TUC was proved to be right when this, in fact, happened less than a month after the National government was formed.

Similarly, no member of the Labour Cabinet argued that economies of less than £76 million were required to keep the pound's parity. Indeed ten of MacDonald's colleagues had, on the night of Sunday 23 August, actually voted with him in favour of the full economies, which, of course, included a 10 per cent cut in unemployment pay. They included Snowden, J.H. Thomas and Lord Sankey (the Lord Chancellor) who joined MacDonald's National government. But they also included Passfield (Sidney Webb), Wedgwood-Benn, Lees-Smith, Miss Bondfield and Herbert Morrison, all of whom went into opposition, with almost the entire Labour Party, when the National government was formed. Every member of the Labour Cabinet was committed to cuts of £56,375,000, even though they realised that this figure would not be sufficient to raise the international loan which all believed to be essential if calamity were to be averted. At MacDonald's suggestion, on Saturday 22 August all the members of the Labour Cabinet were united in agreeing that the Opposition leaders and the bankers should be approached to see whether economies of £76 million would be acceptable to them, provided that it was made clear that the Cabinet *had made no firm commitment to achieve this figure*. In retrospect it is difficult to understand why the minority of nine in the Labour Cabinet agreed to this question being posed at all to the Opposition leaders and the bankers, since, if they were, in any event, determined to resign if £20 million (largely representing the 10 per cent cut in unemployment benefit) were added to the economies which had been agreed by everybody, the Labour Cabinet would cease to exist. If this was the case, the asking of the question was quite pointless.

For MacDonald, the agreement by the Labour Cabinet to this question being posed must have appeared as a chink of light. When the Labour Cabinet met at 7 p.m. on Sunday 23 August it adjourned at 7.45 p.m. in order to wait to hear whether economies of £76 million would be acceptable to the Federal Reserve Bank of America. For an hour and a half Ministers walked up and down the garden of 10 Downing Street waiting for the reply. Why did not the nine, for whom these economies were unacceptable, write out their letters of resignation, since the answer, from their point of view, was irrelevant? When the answer did come and an indication was given in principle that the economies would probably be acceptable to the bankers, Sir Ernest Harvey, the Deputy Governor of the Bank of England, who was waiting outside the Cabinet Room at 9.15 p.m., having given the message to the Prime Minister, recalled that 'pandemonium' seemed to have broken out in the Cabinet meeting. But, what was the pandemonium about? The Cabinet minutes state:

The Prime Minister informed the Cabinet that a situation had now been faced of a peculiarly difficult character because, if the Labour Party was not prepared to join the Conservatives and Liberal Parties in accepting the proposals as a whole, the conditions mentioned in Mr Harrison's [The President of the Reserve Bank] letter would not be fulfilled . . . There was, as yet, no panic at home, but the Prime

Minister warned the Cabinet of the calamitous nature of the consequences which would immediately and inevitably follow from a
financial panic and a flight from the pound . . . When the immediate crisis was over and before Parliament met, it would be possible
to give the Labour Party a full explanation of the circumstances
which had rendered it necessary for the Government to formulate
such a drastic scheme . . . The only alternative was a reduction not
of 10 per cent but of at least 20 per cent, and he could not believe
that the Labour Party would reject the proposals when they knew
the true facts of the position: he was confident, indeed, that a
majority of that Party would accept them. He then pointed out that,
if on this question there were any important resignations, the
Government, as a whole must resign.

It is clear from these minutes that MacDonald was making a final plea
to his Cabinet colleagues to back the proposals. The majority did so,
but the narrowness of the margin – eleven (including his own vote) to
nine plainly made it impossible for the Cabinet to remain in office,
since the nine dissenters were determined to resign rather than accept
the conditions. MacDonald therefore informed his colleagues that he
would inform the King of what had happened and advise him to convene a conference between himself, Baldwin and Samuel in the morning.
The Cabinet agreed to this procedure and asked him to inform the King
that all the Members of the Cabinet had placed their resignations in his
hands.

In fact, by Sunday 23 August, before this vital Cabinet meeting,
MacDonald had already realised that there were three possible courses
of action for himself. He had told the King on that morning that the
Cabinet would in all probability lack the unity to be able to survive. In
this event, he would normally have resigned himself and have gone into
opposition, allowing the Conservatives and Liberals, who, between
them, possessed an overall majority and supported the measures to
carry them out. He would, however, find great difficulty in leading the
Opposition in resisting cuts he believed were both right and inevitable.
It might therefore, he thought, be more honest to resign from the party
leadership as well as the premiership and support the agreed economies
from the Opposition benches. It did not appear to have occurred to

MacDonald that he might remain Prime Minister of an all-party government, until the King had suggested this possibility that morning; and
even then as MacDonald wrote in his diary:

> I explained my hopeless party position if there were any number of
> resignations. He said that he believed I was the only person who
> could carry the country through. I said that did I share his belief I
> should not contemplate what I do, but that I did not share it.

Even when MacDonald did agree to lead a National government he
thought that it would only last for a few weeks. On 24 August, after
MacDonald had seen the King, his son Malcolm noted:

> The King has implored J.R.M. to form a National Government,
> Baldwin and Samuel are both willing to serve under him. This
> Government would last about five weeks to tide over the crisis. It
> would be the end, in his own opinion, of J.R.M.'s career.

Why, then, did MacDonald agree, within a few weeks, to hold a general
election which, under his leadership returned the National government's
supporters (473 of whom were Conservative MPs) with the largest
majority in Parliament in modern times and which reduced the Labour
Party in Parliament to 52? And why did he remain as Prime Minister
for nearly four more years?

There seems to be little doubt that MacDonald was taken completely
unawares by the reaction of the Parliamentary Labour Party to what
had happened. A meeting of the Parliamentary Labour Party was called
for Friday 28 August. MacDonald did not actually see the invitation for
him to attend the meeting until the previous day. He did not attend the
meeting, pleading the need to get away after an unusually burdensome
week. He had, however, already written a personal letter to every
Labour MP, explaining why he had acted as he did, and he received
friendly and understanding replies from many of those who felt unable
to join him, including Ben Tillet, Allen Parkinson, John Arnott, Archie
Gossling, Charles Amman, Clement Attlee, Jack Lawson, Ben Riley,
Ben Turner, W.B. Taylor, James Welsh and Herbert Dunnico.

At the meeting of the Parliamentary Party, which was held on 28

August, Arthur Henderson, the former Foreign Secretary, was elected as Leader of the Parliamentary Party with Clynes, the former Home Secretary, and Graham, the former President of the Board of Trade, as his two deputies. Lord Sankey, the Lord Chancellor, and Malcolm MacDonald, who had become a junior Minister in the National government, did attend and speak, and both were given a not unfriendly hearing. However the Labour Parlaimentary Party decided not only to go into opposition but also, under the influence of the TUC and Ernest Bevin in particular, to engage in battle both against the cut in unemployment benefit and against all the economies which had unanimously been accepted by the former Labour Cabinet. If MacDonald had attended the meeting it must be regarded as unlikely that he could have prevented this decision of the Parliamentary Labour Party from taking place, but his absence made it possible for his enemies in the former Cabinet to say that he was not prepared to face them, an allegation which they were only too ready to make, to cover up their own sudden decision to disown the policies which they had previously supported. While MacDonald was no doubt prepared for his former colleagues to oppose the cut in unemployment pay which had led to the break-up of his government (even though some of them had voted in its favour at the final Cabinet meeting) he never expected them to repudiate *everything*. From this moment bitterness became intense on both sides, and MacDonald began to realise that his original concept of a government which would only last for a few weeks was no longer realistic. How could it be, if the Labour Party and alternative government now opposed all the decisions which were generally thought to be essential if the financial crisis was to be overcome?

It had, of course, always been envisaged that a general election would take place after the National government had taken the necessary steps to overcome the financial crisis. Indeed this was one of the public commitments which was made by the three party leaders when the formation of the National government was announced. It was, however, assumed by all the party leaders that the National government would only last for a few weeks and that when the general election took place each party would fight it separately. The statement from Downing Street, which was issued on 24 August, said, 'When that purpose [the ending of the financial crisis] is achieved, the political parties

will resume their respective positions.' As Snowden wrote in his autobiography, 'I expected that, though we had differed on what, after all,
was a comparatively minor matter, we should be able to resume our
former co-operation in the Labour Party when the emergency legislation had been passed.'

The suggestion that MacDonald was glad or even relieved to be
separated from his former Labour colleagues is not borne out by
impartial contemporary observers. Sir Maurice (later Lord) Hankey,
the Secretary to the Cabinet, had been away during the earlier part of
the crisis and only returned to London at 5 p.m. on Monday 24
August, one hour after the National government had been formed. In
his diary he described his arrival at 10 Downing Street: 'I found him
[MacDonald] in the Cabinet Room with Baldwin and Herbert Samuel
— MacDonald looking very tired and haggard discussing the formation
of the new National Government . . .' Later, on 11 September 1931,
when Parliament had been recalled and the Prime Minister introduced
the Economy Bill, Hankey described MacDonald in this fashion in his
diary:

> The Prime Minister has been very seedy. When under severe nervous
> strain he is apt to vomit, and this leaves him terribly weak. I fear
> he is feeling the break with the rest of the Labour Party very badly
> . . . Snowden who is [as] hard as nails in spite of his physical infir-
> mities, is quite unaffected by his separation from Labour colleagues
> many of whom he despises and dislikes.

On 24 August 1931, after the National government had been formed,
MacDonald wrote to Lady Londonderry, who had become a close
friend of his,

> the general opinion amongst my friends here is that I have commit-
> ted suicide. That being so I shall soon waken in the shades. In any
> event my programme of bowing out has begun with a rogue's march.
> I shall welcome a sight of you again and put on a collar and shirt
> which will hide the hangman's rope around my neck.

On 8 September, the day when Parliament was recalled, MacDonald wrote to Lady Londonderry again:

> The political situation is full of currents and counter currents,
> reasonable and unreasonable, so how long we shall last I know not
> ... In one hour I leave for the House of Commons. Work has been
> so heavy that I have not been able to see Charlie [Lord Londonderry]
> but will do so soon. I wonder if I shall make a mess of it today. I
> am unhappy and wish it were over.

MacDonald wrote in his private diary on the same day: 'Labour Members behaved badly. How could one once ever free from this ill assorted body join it again?'; and 'Tories in the crowd from the inside are even worse than from the outside.'

It is not unreasonable to attribute much of MacDonald's unhappiness to his growing realisation that his breach with the Labour Party had become permanent. Not only had Arthur Henderson supplanted him as Leader of the Labour Party, which was still the largest party in the House of Commons, but on 27 August a general manifesto had been issued by the TUC, the National Executive of the Labour Party and the Consultative Committee of the Parliamentary Labour Party which disowned all the government economies, and in fact adopted virtually all the proposals which had been put forward to the Labour government by the TUC on 20 August. This manifesto had been overwhelmingly endorsed by the meeting of the Parliamentary Labour Party on 28 August. On 30 August the executive of the Seaham Constituency Labour Party had passed a resolution to put to a full delegate meeting in September asking MacDonald to resign his seat. On 12 September this resolution was carried by the narrow margin of 40 votes to 39.

On 10 September Snowden had presented his budget, which included cuts in expenditure of £70 million, to the House of Commons (only £14 million more than the figure accepted by the Labour Cabinet). On 8 September the new National government had won a vote of confidence in the House of Commons by 309 votes to 249. Twelve Labour MPs had voted with the government and five had abstained.

The formation of the National government and the balanced budget had, however, not helped the pound for more than a few days. On 16 September the Bank of England lost £5 million; on the 17th £10

million and on the 18th nearly £18 million. On 19 September Sir
Ernest Harvey and the Bank of England advised MacDonald and
Snowden that there was no alternative except for Britain to abandon
the gold standard. On Monday 21 September legislation was passed in
all its stages through Parliament which relieved the Bank of England of
its obligations under the 1925 Gold Standard Act. This was exactly
twenty-eight days after the formation of the National government,
whose principal purpose had been to avoid this action.

The arguments put forward by the TUC and Ernest Bevin in particular had proved to be right. A budget deficit was irrelevant, since all the
leading industrial countries were running such deficits. From the start,
Ernest Bevin had maintained that the need was for expenditure on
modernising industry, international action to raise the world level of
wholesale prices, the devaluation of the pound, and the introduction of
a revenue tariff. The third proposal had been forced upon the National
government which was shortly, also, to adopt the fourth. Where then
did this leave MacDonald?

Lord Davidson in his draft memoirs minuted a conversation which
he had held on 27 September with Sir Ralph Glynn, a Conservative
MP who had become one of MacDonald's Parliamentary Private Secre-
taries.

> From our conversation, I came definitely to the conclusion that now
> we are off the Gold Standard, Ramsay and Thomas may wish to seek
> re-entry into the Socialist Party, if, as seems clear, Henderson after a
> very short spell as Leader prefers the power of the 'Party Boss' and
> would therefore be willing to resume his old position.

The following day MacDonald, Snowden, Thomas and Sankey and all
other Labour MPs or Ministers who had joined or supported the
National government were expelled from the Labour Party. This made
it impossible for them to rejoin it, though it must be added that the
bitterness which had been engendered between MacDonald and his
former Labour Cabinet colleagues would in any event have made such
a reconciliation most unlikely.

The first reference to a possible general election which appeared in
the Cabinet minutes was on 17 September. The Prime Minister reported

a deterioration in the financial situation and an increase of withdrawal of funds from London during the previous few days. In Item (5) of the Prime Minister's statement, MacDonald said that the Bank had advised that the financial world had been a good deal upset when the statement had been made that the National government was only to be short-lived. The Prime Minister went on to say, according to the Cabinet Minutes:

> While disclaiming any right to an opinion on political events, the representatives of the Bank, when pressed as to their view of what the American and French Banking interests would be likely to consider would provide sufficient security for further credits, had indicated that a General Election in which the three parties were acting individually would not be regarded as providing sufficient certainty for the establishment of a stable Government as the result. An appeal to the electorate by a National Government on national policy devised to rectify the financial situation was more likely to be regarded favourably abroad.

The expulsion of the Labour members of the National government from the Labour Party eleven days later was a watershed. Until then there is reason to think that MacDonald had hoped that he might broaden the base of the government by the inclusion of Henderson and Graham. MacDonald's private diary referred to talks having taken place between Thomas and Henderson about this. However, the total repudiation by the ex-Ministers of the economies which had provisionally been agreed by the Labour Cabinet must have been seen by both sides as making any future relationship between them impossible.

The advice given by the Bank of England, together with the abandonment by Britain of the gold standard, the conduct of the ex-Ministers and his own expulsion from the Labour Party probably led MacDonald to decide at the end of September that the National government must fight the general election as a united team. None of these factors could have been predicted on 24 August when the contrary pledge was given. One difficulty remained. Lloyd George was implacably opposed to a general election. In all probability this opposition was greeted by Sir Herbert Samuel and Sir John Simon with relief.

However, the possibility of including a revenue tariff in the election programme of the National government still remained. A compromise was only reached between the Liberals and their other colleagues at a Cabinet meeting presided over by the Prime Minister on 5 October, only two days before the dissolution of Parliament was announced. MacDonald wrote in his private diary on 5 October: 'It is impossible not to go on without an election. I tried it on at the Cabinet and Thomas, in a thoughtless outburst, played into the hands of the Tories and encouraged them to offer resignation or examination. I believe Chamberlain scribbled a note to Thomas suggesting resignation.' On 6 October he wrote of the Conservatives 'not much "national view" about their machine majors. Never let it be said that the Tory machine had a glimmer of national duty and sacrifice.' On 7 October his entry was even more pathetic:

> It is all terrible but what could have been done? The people I care for most in my life suspect me and are confused. That cuts me to my heart. Will the old relations and affections return? I shall try but the machine Labour men will stand in the way.

Polling day was on 28 October 1931: 473 Conservatives, 35 Liberal Nationals, 33 Liberals, 13 National Labour and 2 National members of Parliament were elected. The Opposition consisted of 52 Labour MPs and four Independent Liberals (all members of the Lloyd George family). Every former Labour Cabinet Minister was defeated, with the exception of George Lansbury. The Labour Party had been destroyed for fourteen years and MacDonald had been the reluctant executioner. On 29 October MacDonald revealed his deep distress in the privacy of his diary:

> My work is to be difficult in all conscience with this enormous Tory majority. At the moment I am most grieved that so many good men and women are out, who ought to be in. The Conservative Head Office pretended to do what it never did and indeed played a sharp game and saw its advantage and took it and, unfortunately the size of the majority has weakened my position. Once again I record that no honest man should trust in too gentlemanly a code in Conservative

wire pullers.

MacDonald's tragedy was a personal one. The National government which he thought (and was persuaded) was essential for him to form and lead in order to save the pound had been unable to do this. The cause for the run on the pound was nothing to do with the need to have a balanced budget, over which the Labour government resigned. The truth was that Britain should never have attempted to restore the pound to its pre-1914 level. Britain went off gold without any of the disasters which had been predicted. MacDonald could, in a different context, have echoed Nurse Edith Cavell's immortal phrase: 'Patriotism is not enough.' He had, as he thought, put country before party. He did not realise at the time that the sacrifice was unnecessary.

APPENDIX I: CABINET MEMBERS, AUGUST — OCTOBER 1931

(1) The Labour Cabinet, August 1931

The Rt. Hon. J. Ramsay MacDonald, MP, Prime Minister and First Lord of the Treasury

The Rt. Hon. Philip Snowden, MP, Chancellor of the Exchequer

The Rt. Hon. Arthur Henderson, MP, Secretary of State for Foreign Affairs

The Rt. Hon. Lord Sankey, Lord Chancellor

The Rt. Hon. Lord Parmoor, Lord President of the Council

The Rt. Hon. J.H. Thomas, MP, Secretary of State for Dominion Affairs

The Rt. Hon. Lord Passfield, Secretary of State for the Colonies

The Rt. Hon. J.R. Clynes, MP, Secretary of State for Home Affairs

The Rt. Hon. W. Wedgwood-Benn, MP, Secretary of State for India

The Rt. Hon. Tom Shaw, MP, Secretary of State for War

The Rt. Hon. Lord Amulree, Secretary of State for Air

The Rt. Hon. Arthur Greenwood, MP, Minister of Health

The Rt. Hon. Margaret Bondfield, MP, Minister of Labour

The Rt. Hon. Christopher Addison, MP, Minister of Agriculture and Fisheries

The Rt. Hon. H.B. Lees-Smith, MP, President of the Board of Education

The Rt. Hon. W. Graham, MP, President of the Board of Trade

The Rt. Hon. A.V. Alexander, MP, First Lord of the Admiralty

The Rt. Hon. William Adamson, MP, Secretary of State for Scotland

The Rt. Hon. George Lansbury, MP, First Commissioner of Works

The Rt. Hon. Herbert Morrison, MP, Minister of Transport

The Rt. Hon. T. Johnston, MP, Lord Privy Seal

(2) The National Government Cabinet, 26 August 1931

The Rt. Hon. J. Ramsay MacDonald, MP, Prime Minister and First Lord of the Treasury (National Labour)

The Rt. Hon. Stanley Baldwin, MP, Lord President of the Council

(Conservative)

The Rt. Hon. Philip Snowden, MP, Chancellor of the Exchequer (National Labour)

The Rt. Hon. Sir Herbert Samuel, MP, Secretary of State for Home Affairs (Liberal)

The Rt. Hon. Lord Sankey, Lord Chancellor (National Labour)

The Most Hon. The Marquess of Reading, Secretary of State for Foreign Affairs (Liberal)

The Rt. Hon. Sir Samuel Hoare, MP, Secretary of State for India (Conservative)

The Rt. Hon. J.H. Thomas, MP, Secretary of State for Dominion Affairs and Secretary of State for the Colonies (National Labour)

The Rt. Hon. Neville Chamberlain, MP, Minister of Health (Conservative)

The Rt. Hon. Sir Philip Cunliffe-Lister, MP, President of the Board of Trade (Conservative)

(3)   The National Government Cabinet after the General Election, October 1931

The Rt. Hon. J. Ramsay MacDonald, MP, Prime Minister and First Lord of the Treasury (National Labour)

The Rt. Hon. Stanley Baldwin, MP, Lord President of the Council (Conservative)

The Rt. Hon. Neville Chamberlain, MP, Chancellor of the Exchequer (Conservative)

The Rt. Hon. Sir Herbert Samuel, MP, Secretary of State for Home Affairs (Liberal)

The Rt. Hon. Lord Sankey, Lord Chancellor (National Labour)

The Rt. Hon. Viscount Hailsham, Secretary of State for War (Conservative)

The Rt. Hon. Sir John Simon, MP, Secretary of State for Foreign Affairs (Liberal National)

The Rt. Hon. Sir Samuel Hoare, MP, Secretary of State for India (Conservative)

The Rt. Hon. J.H. Thomas, MP, Secretary of State for Dominion Affairs (National Labour)

The Rt. Hon. Sir Philip Cunliffe-Lister, MP, Secretary of State for the

Colonies (Conservative)

The Most. Hon. the Marquess of Londonderry, Secretary of State for Air (Conservative)

The Rt. Hon. Sir Archibald Sinclair, MP, Secretary of State for Scotland (Liberal)

The Rt. Hon. Sir Edward Hilton-Young, MP, Minister of Health (Conservative)

The Rt. Hon. Walter Runciman, MP, President of the Board of Trade (Liberal National)

The Rt. Hon. Viscount Snowden, Lord Privy Seal (National Labour)

The Rt. Hon. Sir Bolton Eyres-Monsell, MP, First Lord of the Admiralty (Conservative)

The Rt. Hon. Sir Donald Maclean, MP, President of the Board of Education (Liberal)

The Rt. Hon. Sir John Gilmour, MP, Minister of Agriculture and Fisheries (Conservative)

The Rt. Hon. Sir Henry Betterton, MP, Minister of Labour (Conservative)

The Rt. Hon. W. Ormsby-Gore, MP, First Commissioner of Works (Conservative)

APPENDIX II: MINUTES OF THE LABOUR CABINET AT WHICH THE RESIGNATION OF THE LABOUR GOVERN-MENT WAS DECIDED, SUNDAY 23 AUGUST 1931

SECRET

Cabinet 46 (31)

Conclusions of a Meeting of the Cabinet held at 10 Downing Street, SW1, on Sunday 23rd August 1931 at 7 p.m.

Present

The Rt. Hon. J. Ramsay MacDonald, MP, Prime Minister in the Chair

The Rt. Hon. Philip Snowden, MP, Chancellor of the Exchequer

The Rt. Hon. J.H. Thomas, MP, Secretary of State for Dominion Affairs

The Rt. Hon. Lord Sankey, GBE, Lord Chancellor

The Rt. Hon. W. Wedgwood-Benn, DSO, DFC, MP, Secretary of State for India

The Rt. Hon. Lord Amulree, GBE, KC, Secretary of State for Air

The Rt. Hon. Margaret Bondfield, MP, Minister of Labour

The Rt. Hon. H.B. Lees-Smith, MP, President of the Board of Education

The Rt. Hon. A.V. Alexander, MP, First Lord of the Admiralty

The Rt. Hon. George Lansbury, MP, First Commissioner of Works

The Rt. Hon. Arthur Henderson, MP, Secretary of State for Foreign Affairs

The Rt. Hon. Lord Passfield, Secretary of State for the Colonies

The Rt. Hon. J.R. Clynes, MP, Secretary of State for Home Affairs

The Rt. Hon. Tom Shaw, MP, Secretary of State for War

The Rt. Hon. Arthur Greenwood, MP, Minister of Health

The Rt. Hon. Christopher Addison, MP, Minister of Agriculture and Fisheries

The Rt. Hon. W. Graham, MP, President of the Board of Trade

The Rt. Hon. William Adamson, MP, Secretary of State for Scotland

The Rt. Hon. Herbert Morrison, MP, Minister of Transport

The Rt. Hon. T. Johnston, MP, Lord Privy Seal
R.B. Howarth, CB, CMG, Deputy Secretary

Financial Situation The Bankers' Reply (Prev Ret Cab 45 (31) meeting conclusion No. 2 on page 4)

In pursuance of the conclusion referred to in the margin, the Cabinet met to receive a report from the Prime Minister in regard to the reply of the Bankers. After reminding the Cabinet that the Chancellor of the Exchequer and himself had seen the representatives of the Bank of England on the previous afternoon, and had ascertained from them that after getting in touch with Mr. Harrison they would communicate with him again, the Prime Minister informed the Cabinet that he had received at 10 p.m. on the previous evening a telephone message from Sir E. Harvey, to the effect that Mr. Harrison had expressed his own personal opinion that, if a further £20 million gross was added to the list of economies, made up as to £12¼ million by a 10 per cent reduction in Unemployment Insurance benefit and as to £7¾ million in other ways, the proposals as a whole would be satisfactory from the point of view of the proposed loan, but that he must first confer with the financial interests responsible for raising the money in New York. Meetings for this purpose had been held that day (August 23rd) in New York and London, and although no answer had yet been received from New York it was confidently expected that a reply would come a little later in the evening. The Prime Minister added that he had not again seen the Leaders of the Opposition Parties, but he reminded the Cabinet that those Leaders had undertaken to support the proposals if the letter were satisfactory to the financial interests.

The Prime Minister then informed the Cabinet that he had seen His Majesty and had advised him to acquaint himself with the views of the Leaders of the Conservative and Liberal Parties on the situation. The question before the Cabinet was whether, in the event of the reply from New York being satisfactory they were now prepared to add the 10 per cent reduction in Unemployment Insurance benefit, and the other additional economies, making in all £20 million gross to the programme which had already been approved.

Some discussion took place as to the precise position regarding the

Parliamentary situation, and on this point the Prime Minister reminded the Cabinet that when he and the Chancellor of the Exchequer met the Leaders of the Opposition Parties he had been assured in effect that they would be ready, by means of a Parliamentary agreement, to accept and support the proposals provided that the financial interests were satisfied as to their sufficiency to meet the emergency. He, the Prime Minister, had made it clear that he interpreted the expression 'Parliamentary agreement' to mean that both Oppositions would facilitate the passage of the Government's proposals, but that, if for example the Oppositions carried a motion to increase the Unemployment Insurance benefit from 10 per cent to 20 per cent, the Government would then be at liberty to regard the vote as one of 'no confidence'. He did not however consider that the Parliamentary situation presented any real difficulty.

At 7.45 p.m. the Cabinet adjourned to await the message from New York, and resumed at 9.10 p.m. when the Prime Minister read to the Cabinet a message which had been addressed personally to him by Mr. Harrison. For a copy of this message see Appendix. The Prime Minister informed the Cabinet that he had ascertained from the Deputy Governor of the Bank of England that they had sounded out in strict confidence certain important and influential financial interests in the City of London, all of which were prepared to support the scheme. The Bank of England was also satisfied as to the technical aspects of the financial proposals for the short term credit mentioned in the message and thought that the amount suggested would suffice, provided that Parliament passed the legislation necessary to secure budgetary equilibrium within a strictly limited time.

With regard to the concluding paragraph of the message, the Prime Minister pointed out that, as the Opposition Parties had undertaken to support the Government's proposals, the condition laid down in that paragraph might be regarded as fulfilled.

He most sincerely hoped that the Cabinet would now accept the proposals as a whole. If however the Cabinet were unable to accept them, then it was clear that the loan which was essential to avert the crisis, would not be forthcoming and it was unthinkable that the Government should remain in Office and prevent some other Administration being given the opportunity of deciding that the money should be found.

The Chancellor of the Exchequer expressed himself as generally satisfied from the technical point of view with the proposals of the American financial interest as set out in Mr. Harrison's message, and the Prime Minister again stressed his hope that, provided that there was no Treasury objection to the 'Harrison terms', the Cabinet would accept the full proposals including the 10 per cent cut in Unemployment Insurance benefit. It was not anticipated that there would be any difficulty in securing the co-operation of French financial interests in the financial proposals.

The Prime Minister informed the Cabinet that a situation had now to be faced of a peculiarly difficult character because, if the Labour Party was not prepared to join with the Conservative and Liberal Parties in accepting the proposals as a whole, the condition mentioned in Mr. Harrison's message regarding a national agreement would not be fulfilled.

So far as he was concerned, he was strongly in favour of such acceptance while at the same time making clear that the scheme represented the extreme limit to which he was prepared to go.

The Country was suffering from lack of confidence abroad. There was, as yet, no panic at home but the Prime Minister warned the Cabinet of the calamitous nature of the consequences which would immediately and inevitably follow from a financial panic and a flight from the pound. No one could be blind to the very great political difficulties in which the giving effect to the proposals as a whole would involve the Government.

But when the immediate crisis was over and before Parliament met, it would be possible to give the Labour Party that full explanation of the circumstances which had rendered it necessary for the Government to formulate such a drastic scheme, which could not be given at the moment. The only alternative was a reduction of not 10 per cent, but of at least 20 per cent, and he could not believe that the Labour Party would reject the proposals when they knew the true facts of the position: he was confident, indeed, that a majority of the Party would accept them. A scheme which inflicted reductions and burdens in almost every other direction, but made no appreciable cut in Unemployment Insurance benefit, would alienate much support and lose the Party their moral prestige which was one of their greatest assets. In conclusion, the Prime Minister said that it must be admitted that the proposals as a whole represented the negation of everything that the Labour Party stood for, and yet he was absolutely satisfied that it was necessary in the national interests to implement them if the country was to be secured. He then pointed out that, if on this question there were any important resignations, the Government as a whole must resign.

Each member of the Cabinet then expressed his views on the question of the inclusion, or otherwise, in the proposals of the 10 per cent reduction in Unemployment Insurance benefit. In the course of these expressions of view, indications were given that, while a majority of the Cabinet favoured the inclusion in the economy proposals of the 10 per cent reduction in Unemployment Insurance benefit, the adoption of this as part and parcel of the scheme would involve the resignation of certain Ministers from the Government.

In these circumstances the Prime Minister informed the Cabinet that he proposed to acquaint His Majesty at once with the situation which had arisen, and to advise him to hold a Conference with Mr. Baldwin, Sir H. Samuel and himself on the following morning. The Cabinet agreed to this proposal, and also authorised the Prime Minister to inform His Majesty that all Cabinet Ministers had placed their resignations in the Prime Minister's hands. The Prime Minister left the meeting of the Cabinet at 10.10 p.m.

The Prime Minister returned from Buckingham Palace at about 10.40 p.m. and stated to the Cabinet that he had informed His Majesty of the situation, namely that, while the Government had agreed that the Budget should be balanced, they had been unable to reach agreement on proposals to deal effectively with the existing financial emergency, and accordingly that it was impossible for them to continue in office as a united Cabinet. He had then advised His Majesty that he should accord an Audience to Mr. Baldwin, Sir Herbert Samuel and himself on the following morning, and His Majesty had been pleased to fix 10 a.m. as the time for this Audience.

The Cabinet agreed:

(i) that no announcement should be issued to the Press;

(ii) that the Prime Minister should inform the Leaders of the Opposition

Parties forthwith of the nature of the message which he had received from Mr. Harrison;

(iii) to leave the question of summoning Parliament in the hands of the Prime Minister;

(iv) that a further meeting of the Cabinet should be held on Monday next, August 24th at No. 10 Downing Street, at 12 noon but that no formal notice of this meeting should be issued.

Future Arrangements Regarding Ministerial Responsibility

In the course of the discussion referred to in the previous conclusion the Prime Minister reminded the Cabinet that it was the constitutional practice that, after resignation, each Minister continued to perform the purely formal functions of his office until the appointment of his successor, but abstained from questions of policy. Ministers concerned would receive notice as to the arrangements for the surrender of the Seals of Office.

The Cabinet took note of the Prime Minister's statement.

APPENDIX III: THE TEXT OF THE PERSONAL MESSAGE FROM MR GEORGE HARRISON TO THE PRIME MINISTER, 23 AUGUST 1931

We are considering very carefully the tentative suggestion made by the Deputy Governor of the Bank as to the bare possibility of the British Government desiring to arrange some form of joint French and American credit, but it is quite impossible to give any assurance today. Please tell your friends in the event that they should desire financial co-operation, we shall always do our utmost to meet their wishes. If the suggestion were to take the shape of a public loan offering, we are confident that until Parliament convene and act and until we have had an opportunity to feel out our investment community, we could render no favourable opinion whatsoever. If the suggestion, however, were to take the form of a short-term Treasury operation that would be less difficult and if the British Government should canvass amongst ourselves we would take up the matter vigorously tomorrow morning and be able to give you an answer by our closing time tomorrow afternoon.

Kindly let us know, subsequent to the result of the Cabinet Meeting which you say will be held this evening whether the Government wishes us to explore promptly this possibility. The furthest we have gone today is to discuss merely amongst ourselves the possibility of a short credit in this market of $100,000,000 to $150,000,000 and we have as before indicated that as a condition the French market will do an equivalent amount. When we state a short term we have roughly in mind 90 day Treasury Bills subject to renewal for an inclusive period of one year.

In the foregoing we have as always given you the precise trend of our thoughts. Let us know promptly as above indicated what the Government's desires are and within 24 hours we shall be able to give you our final judgement.

Are we right in assuming that the programme under consideration will have the sincere approval and support of the Bank of England and the City generally and thus go a long way towards restoring internal confidence in Great Britain?

Of course our ability to do anything depends on the response of public opinion, particularly in Great Britain, to the Government's announcement of the programme.

APPENDIX IV: MINUTES OF THE FINAL MEETING OF THE LABOUR CABINET, 24 AUGUST 1931

Cabinet 47 (31)

Conclusions of a Meeting of the Cabinet held at 10 Downing Street SW1 on Monday August 24th at 12 Noon.

Present

The Rt. Hon. J. Ramsay MacDonald, MP, Prime Minister, in the Chair

The Rt. Hon. Philip Snowden, MP, Chancellor of the Exchequer
The Rt. Hon. J.H. Thomas, MP, Secretary of State for Dominion Affairs
The Rt. Hon. Lord Sankey, GBE, Lord Chancellor
The Rt. Hon. W. Wedgwood-Benn, DSO, DFC, MP, Secretary of State for India
The Rt. Hon. Lord Amulree, GBE, KC, Secretary of State for Air
The Rt. Hon. Margaret Bondfield, MP, Minister of Labour
The Rt. Hon. H.B. Lees-Smith, MP, President of the Board of Education
The Rt. Hon. A.V. Alexander, MP, First Lord of the Admiralty
The Rt. Hon. George Lansbury, MP, First Commissioner of Works
The Rt. Hon. Arthur Henderson, MP, Secretary of State for Foreign Affairs
The Rt. Hon. Lord Passfield, Secretary of State for the Colonies
The Rt. Hon. J.R. Clynes, MP, Secretary of State for Home Affairs
The Rt. Hon. Tom Shaw, MP, Secretary of State for War
The Rt. Hon. Arthur Greenwood, MP, Minister of Health
The Rt. Hon. Christopher Addison, MP, Minister of Agriculture and Fisheries
The Rt. Hon. W. Graham, MP, President of the Board of Trade
The Rt. Hon. William Adamson, MP, Secretary of State for Scotland
The Rt. Hon. Herbert Morrison, MP, Minister of Transport
The Rt. Hon. T. Johnston, MP, Lord Privy Seal
R.B. Howarth, CB, CMG, Deputy Secretary

The Financial Position Resignation of the Government

(1) The Prime Minister informed the Cabinet that, as a result of the failure to reach agreement on the previous day, the financial position had greatly deteriorated and the situation was now one of the gravest possible character.

As had then been arranged His Majesty had received Mr. Baldwin, Sir Herbert Samuel and himself in audience that morning, and it was quite clear that no useful purpose would be served by consideration of any question other than that of saving the country from financial collapse. The proposal was that His Majesty would invite certain individuals, as individuals, to take upon their shoulders the burden of carrying on the Government, and Mr. Baldwin and Sir Herbert Samuel had stated that they were prepared to act accordingly. The Prime Minister then stated that he proposed to tender to His Majesty the resignation of the Government. He had not failed to present the case against his participation in the proposed Administration but, in view of the gravity of the situation, he felt that there was no other course open to him than to assist in the formation of a National Government on a comprehensive basis for the purpose of meeting the present emergency. The new Cabinet would be a very small one of about 12 Ministers and the Administration would not exist for a period longer than was necessary to dispose of the emergency and that when that purpose had been achieved the Political Parties would resume their respective positions. The Administration would not be a Coalition Government in the usual sense of the term but a Government of co-operation for this one purpose.

It had been agreed that at the General Election, which would follow the end of the emergency period, there would be no 'coupons', pacts or other Party arrangements. During the emergency period efforts would be made to avoid contests at by-elections but, if such contests took place it would be open to the Leaders of the Conservative and Liberal Parties to send letters to their candidates.

While the Administration held office it was not proposed that there should be any Party legislation, but efforts would be made to arrange for the passage into law of measures in regard to which the three parties were in substantial agreement. The Prime Minister gave an example of such Legislation – The London Traffic Bill – and intimated that he thought that arrangements could be made to secure the passage of that Bill into law,

The Prime Minister added that he had obtained assurances to the effect that the general scheme of economies to be placed before Parliament by the new Administration would be on the basis of the proposals which had been submitted to the Bankers, including the 10 per cent cut in Unemployment Insurance. In effect there would be no serious departure from the Scheme which at their Meeting on August 23rd (Cabinet 45 (31)) the Cabinet had authorised the Chancellor and himself to submit tentatively to the Leaders of the Opposition Parties and to the Bankers.

In reply to an enquiry about the approximate date of the General Election, the Prime Minister said that nothing whatever had, as yet, been decided about this matter.

The Cabinet agreed –

(1) that the Prime Minister should place the resignation of the Government in the hands of His Majesty the King that afternoon

(2) that it hoped that arrangements could be made so that Ministers might surrender their Seals possibly on Tuesday August 25th and in any case with the least possible delay

(3) to adhere to the procedure of their predecessors in regard to Cabinet Documents: that is to say, Ministers should retain such Cabinet documents as they desired, on the understanding that as ex-Ministers they should have access to Cabinet Minutes and other documents issued during their period of office.

Re-circulation of Certain Cabinet Documents

(2) Several Ministers of the Cabinet drew attention to the fact that the copies of most secret papers (C.P. 203 (31) and C.P. 203 (31) (Revise) – the report of the Cabinet Committee on the Report of the Committee on National Expenditure) had been returned by all Members of the Cabinet to the Deputy Secretary and that without them it would be difficult, if not impossible for individual Members of the Cabinet hereafter to know precisely how far they were committed with regard to

the various proposals set out in the documents in question.

The Cabinet agreed:

That there should be returned to each Cabinet Minister his copy of the most secret papers (C.P. 203 (31) and C.P. 203 (31) (Revise))

Thanks to the Prime Minister

(3) On the motion of the Lord Chancellor, the Cabinet placed on record their warm appreciation of the great kindness, consideration and courtesy invariably shown by the Prime Minister when presiding over their meetings and conducting the business of the Cabinet.

APPENDIX V: PAPER SUBMITTED TO THE CABINET ON 19 AUGUST 1931 AND RETURNED BY EACH MEMBER TO THE DEPUTY SECRETARY TO THE CABINET AFTER THE CONCLUSION OF THE MEETING

MOST SECRET
C.P. 201 (31)

Cabinet
Committee on the Report of the Committee on National Expenditure

Deficit	£170,000,000
Economies	£ 78,575,000
	£ 91,425,000

Increased revenue		£m
Increased direct taxes		62
Increased indirect taxes		26.5
		88.5
Economies		
Unemployment insurance		
Anomalies	3	
Reduction to 26 weeks	8+	
Increase of Contributions	15*	28.5
Premium	2.5	
Transitional Benefit		20
Education		11.4†
Roads		7.8
Services		9
Police		0.5
Forestry		0.5
Unemployments Grants Committee		0.5
Agriculture		0.6
Agriculture (Scotland)		0.075
Health		1.7
Empire Marketing Board		0.25
Colonial Development		0.25
Miscellaneous		2.5
Total less £5m in respect of U.I.		83.575
Contributions falling on budget		5
		78.575

+ This is the figure in the May Report. If no reduction in rates of benefit is made the figure should become £10 million.
* £5m of this from the Budget.
† England and Wales only.

APPENDIX VI: PAPER CONTAINING THE ECONOMIES WHICH HAD BEEN AGREED BY THE CABINET BY 21 AUGUST 1931 AND WHICH WAS RETURNED TO THE DEPUTY SECRETARY TO THE CABINET AT THE CONCLUSION OF THE CABINET MEETING ON 21 AUGUST BY EACH MEMBER OF THE CABINET

MOST SECRET
C.P. 203 (31) Revise

Cabinet
Committee on the Report of the Committee on National Expenditure

Deficit	£170,000,000
Economies as below	£ 56,375,000
	£113,625,000

Increased Revenue	**£m**
Increased direct taxes	62
Increased indirect taxes	26.5
	88.5

Economies

Unemployment Insurance (Relief to Exchequer)		
Anomalies Act just passed	3	
Increase of Contribution (to 10d)	10 (net) +	
Increase of Contributions (additional 2d) on insured persons in work	4	
Needs Test for Transitional Benefit, up to	5	22

Note With a live Register of 3,000,000 the remaining charge to the Exchequer in 1932/3 for Unemployment Insurance will be £93,000,000.

Education England and Wales	9.4
Education Scotland	1.3
Roads	7.8
Services	9
Police	0.5
Forestry	0.5
Unemployments Grants Committee	0.5

Agriculture (Scotland)	0.075
Agriculture	0.6
Health	1.7
Empire Marketing Board	0.25
Colonial Development	0.25
Miscellaneous	2.5
	56.375

+ Total increase of Contributions £15m less £5m falling on Exchequer.

BIBLIOGRAPHY

Amery, B.S., *My Political Life and Volumes*
Attlee, Earl, *As it Happened*
Avon, the Earl of, *Facing the Dictators*
Bassett, R.J., *Nineteen Thirty One Political Crisis*
Beaverbrook, Lord, *Men and Power*
Bewdley, Earl Baldwin of, *My Father, the True Story*
Birkenhead, Lord, *Halifax, the Life of Lord Halifax*
——, *Frederick Edwin 1st Earl of Birkenhead*
Blake, Robert, *The Unknown Prime Minister*
Boothby, R., *I Fight to Live*
Bullock, Alan, *Life and Times of Ernest Bevin* (2 volumes)
Butler, Lord, *The Art of the Possible*
Cecil, Viscount, *All the Way*
Citrine, Lord, *Men and Work*
Clynes, J.R., *Memoirs* (2 volumes)
Cole, Margaret, *The Diaries of Beatrice Webb*
Cooper, Duff, *Old Men Forget*
Cross, J.A., *Sir Samuel Hoare*
Dugdale, Blanche, *Arthur James Balfour* (2 volumes)
Elton, Lord, *The Life of Ramsay MacDonald*
Feiling, Keith, *The Life of Neville Chamberlain*
Foot, Michael, *Aneurin Bevan* (Volume 1)
Grigg, P.J. *Prejudice and Judgement*
Hamilton, Mary Agnes, *Ramsay MacDonald*
Home, Lord, *The Way the Wind Blows*
Hyde, Montgomery H., *Neville Chamberlain*
Koss, Stephen, *Asquith*
MacDonald, Malcolm, *Titans and Others*
McKenzie, R. T., *British Political Parties*
Macleod, Iain, *Neville Chamberlain*
Macmillan, Harold, *The Past Masters*
Macneil Weir, J., *The Tragedy of Ramsay MacDonald*

Makintosh, John P., (ed), *British Prime Ministers in the Twentieth Century*

Marquand, David, *Ramsay MacDonald*

Middlemas, Keith and Barnes, John, *Baldwin : A Biography*

Morrison, Herbert, *Herbert Morrison* (Autobiography)

Mosley, Oswald, *My Life*

Muggeridge, Malcolm, *The Thirties*

Nicolson, Sir Harold, *King George V, his Life and Reign*

Owen, Frank, *Tempestuous Journey*

Petrie, Sir Charles, *The Life and Letters of Austen Chamberlain* (2 volumes)

Public Record Office, *Cabinet Minutes and Documents 1923-4, 1929-32*

Rhodes, James, Robert, *Memoirs of a Conservative*

―――, *J.C.C. Davidson's Memoirs and Papers*

―――, *Churchill – a Study in Failure*

Rose, Kenneth, *Superior Person*

Skidelsky, Robert, *Politicians and the Slump*

―――, *Oswald Mosley*

Snowden, Viscount, *An Autobiography* (2 volumes)

Stevenson, John, and Cook, Chris, *The Slump*

Swinton, Viscount, *I Remember*

Taylor, A.J.P., *English History 1914-1945*

Templewood, Viscount, *Nine Troubled Years*

Wheeler Bennett, Sir John, *Sir John Anderson (Lord Waverley)*

Wilson, Harold, *A Prime Minister on Prime Ministers*

Wilson, Trevor, *The Downfall of the Liberal Party*

Winterton, Lord, *Orders of the Day*

Young, G.M., *Stanley Baldwin*

Young, Kenneth, *Baldwin*

INDEX

For Product Safety Concerns and Information please contact our EU
representative GPSR@taylorandfrancis.com
Taylor & Francis Verlag GmbH, Kaufingerstraße 24, 80331 München, Germany